Learning versus the Common Core

FORERUNNERS: IDEAS FIRST
FROM THE UNIVERSITY OF MINNESOTA PRESS

Original e-works to spark new scholarship

FORERUNNERS: IDEAS FIRST is a thought-in-process series of break-through digital works. Written between fresh ideas and finished books, Forerunners draws on scholarly work initiated in notable blogs, social media, conference plenaries, journal articles, and the synergy of academic exchange. This is gray literature publishing: where intense thinking, change, and speculation take place in scholarship.

Nicholas Tampio
Learning versus the Common Core

Kathryn Yusoff
A Billion Black Anthropocenes or None

Kenneth J. Saltman
The Swindle of Innovative Educational Finance

Ginger Nolan
The Neocolonialism of the Global Village

Joanna Zylinska
The End of Man: A Feminist Counterapocalypse

Robert Rosenberger
Callous Objects: Designs against the Homeless

William E. Connolly
**Aspirational Fascism: The Struggle for
Multifaceted Democracy under Trumpism**

Chuck Rybak
UW Struggle: When a State Attacks Its University

Clare Birchall
**Shareveillance: The Dangers of Openly Sharing
and Covertly Collecting Data**

(Continued on page 90)

Learning versus the Common Core

Nicholas Tampio

University of Minnesota Press

MINNEAPOLIS

LONDON

The University of Minnesota Press
111 Third Avenue South, Suite 290
Minneapolis, MN 55401-2520
http://www.upress.umn.edu

Contents

Introduction

ARE YOU A PARENT of children whose education has been impacted by the Common Core? Are you a teacher, a school board member, or an administrator who wants to learn more about the standards and why they are controversial? Are you a journalist or a citizen who wants to understand one of the major developments in recent American history, namely, the creation of a national set of performance expectations in English language arts (ELA) and mathematics? Then you are the intended audience of this book, which collects, thematically, op-eds, blog posts, and magazine articles that I have written about the Common Core and the education reform movement.

The opening section includes two blog posts that explain why my wife and I entered and remain in the fight against the Common Core. The first describes our eldest son's experience in kindergarten when New York started to implement the Common Core. In a flash, our son's Montessori-trained teacher had to stop doing hands-on activities and start using a packaged curriculum aligned to the standards. Like many parents, we protest the Common Core because we have watched it make school a miserable place for our children. A few years later, the local school adopted the New York State Education Department Common Core Curriculum. Common Core proponents say that there is a difference between standards and curriculum. Though I understand that conceptual distinction, the Common Core makes it easier for schools across the country to use scripts that give little freedom to teachers or students.

The second section is on the villains of the Common Core story. Bill and Melinda Gates, the main funders of the Common Core, use their wealth to impose their vision of education on other people's children. David Coleman, the architect of the Common Core, wrote standards that express an antidemocratic philosophy of education premised on regurgitating evidence from an assigned text. Michael Barber is the chief academic officer of Pearson and a theorist of deliverology, the process by which reformers enact change on a large scale even in the face of popular opposition. Arne Duncan, John B. King Jr., Rahm Emmanuel, Andrew Cuomo, and Barack Obama are Democratic Party elites who send their own children to private schools that do not strictly follow the Common Core. And Congress passed the Every Student Succeeds Act of 2015, which prohibits the secretary of education from requiring states to use the Common Core but contains provisions that make it difficult for states to use an alternative to it.

Are the standards themselves the problem? I offer a long answer to that question in my book *Common Core: National Education Standards and the Threat to Democracy* (2018). Here I identify a few problems with the Common Core standards and two other sets of standards aligned with them. The ELA standards require students to "cite specific textual evidence," not think about how the material relates to the world, other things that they have read, or their own lives. The mathematics standards use pretentious language to describe a slow-paced math progression that does not prepare many students for STEM careers. The Next Generation Science Standards are connected to the Common Core and lead to a science education using computer simulations rather than hands-on activities. And the Advanced Placement U.S. History (APUSH) enables one group, the College Board, to hold a de facto monopoly on how honors students learn American history. E. D. Hirsch thinks that the Common Core standards can be saved if they are supplemented with national content standards; I argue that education traditionalists should join forces with education progressives and contest the Common Core with its emphasis on testable skills.

The fourth section considers how the Common Core fits within what Finnish scholar Pasi Sahlberg calls the "global education reform movement" (GERM). The United Nations (UN) has published several recent reports calling for the worldwide adoption of standards-based reform, and reformers use America's middling ranking on the Programme for International Student Assessment (PISA) as proof that the country needs the Common Core. I wrote an article for a Brazilian newspaper arguing why that country should not adopt the National Curricular Base and a blog for an online international relations journal arguing that the United States should not embrace a testing regime similar to the Chinese *gaokao*. Reformers sometimes say that American students need to have more grit; I argue that teaching grit can contribute to an authoritarian political culture wherein young people do what they are told rather than question the status quo.

In the fifth section, I offer concrete advice about what people can do to contest the Common Core and advocate sensible education policies. Parents, educators, and citizens need to forge wide-ranging coalitions to stop systemic education reform. Democrats, Republicans, and Independents got us into the Common Core mess; Democrats, Republicans, and

Independents will have to get us out of it. People need to see the relationship between Common Core testing and the collection of personally identifiable data, including students' moods. Yohuru Williams and I coauthored an article arguing that the civil rights movement ought to oppose the Common Core for narrowing the curriculum, particularly for historically disadvantaged communities. Elites did not want a public debate before states adopted the Common Core as part of their Race to the Top applications; refusing the Common Core tests is one way for parents to signal that they are dissatisfied with the new educational regime. Finally, parents should question when policy makers such as secretary of education Betsy DeVos say that the Common Core is dead; as long as states retain the Common Core ELA anchor standards, Standards of Mathematical Practice, and math progressions, they still follow the Common Core.

In the last essay, I articulate a positive vision of democratic education drawing on the American philosopher John Dewey. Educators should find out what interests children and use that as fuel to inspire them to reach the forefronts of academic knowledge. Schools should be filled with building materials, gardens, woodshops, theaters, art studios, and computer labs and have ample opportunities for students to do field trips and meet with people in the community. A good school has well-trained teachers, small class sizes, a library, a beautiful campus, healthy food, and opportunities for students to do self-directed projects. Presently, schools are teaching a few children to lead and the vast majority to do what they are told. Democratic education means empowering each child to understand how the world works and instilling the confidence to change it.

Why We Fight

Kindergarten, Disrupted

A few years ago, my wife and I walked into a kindergarten classroom where the teacher and a Japanese mother were teaching the kids to fold origami birds. We were impressed to see the children learning about another culture, concentrating for a sustained period of time, developing fine motor skills, and smiling. We bought a house in that school district. My son started kindergarten and, by a marvelous coincidence, was assigned to that teacher. We were delighted as our son planted acorns and watched them grow, studied and replicated the paintings of famous artists, and wrote and drew in journals.

In the middle of the school year, my son's class was selected to pilot a reading program designed to satisfy the Common Core criteria. The teacher started dedicating two hours a day to packaged lesson plans. Rather than giving the students free work choice, in which they build with blocks or paint, the students must sit on the floor while the teacher lectures at them. Rather than tailoring the curriculum to each child, she handed students books from a narrow, predetermined list. Parent volunteers were less welcome in the classroom, and the school district cut funding for kindergarten aides.

The class, in short, shifted from one where teachers, aides, parents, and students worked hard to create a rewarding educational experience to one where the teachers and students used materials designed by a major publishing house.

Many of the aims of the Common Core are admirable. A functioning democracy needs literate citizens. Every young person in our country should be able to read a newspaper, use a computer, do basic math, and so forth. We should be able to evaluate teachers and reward the good ones. The Bush administration (No Child Left Behind) and Obama administration (Race to the Top) have employed language that seems hard to resist.

But we should challenge the drive to uniformity expressed by such programs.

First, we ought to appreciate the reasoning behind America's historical commitment to local control over school districts. America's founders were nervous about the dangers inherent to a strong national government. James Madison, in *Federalist* 10, provided a brilliant argument for why power ought to be divided between branches and layers of government. Sometimes there may be enlightened statesmen or policy makers at the helm. In many cases, however, politicians and bureaucrats will be motivated by self- and group interest. Thus the Constitution ensures that no group can easily assemble great power and, at the same time, that virtually all groups will be able to exercise some power. Public policy will result from endless compromises and negotiations. This framework frustrates efforts to get things done quickly, but it also thwarts efforts by the majority in one policy arena to oppress the minority.

With regard to education, a strong federal policy can help in some instances. But a powerful faction committed to the Common Core can also do mischief. A theme in the Common Core literature is a commitment to the "same goals for all students." Is this a worthy objective? All democratic citizens should have certain minimal skills. But the Common Core runs from kindergarten to twelfth grade, thus teaching more than simple reading or math. Who decides what those same goals should be? Academics from the East Coast? Educators from the Midwest or South? Businessmen or women with no experience teaching? Liberals? Conservatives? Virtually every constituency will be objectionable to someone else in America.

Reasonable people disagree on the goals of education. Rather than try to enforce one pedagogical orthodoxy, we ought to appreciate Madison's insight that America is big enough for many types of social experiment.

A second reason to oppose the Common Core is more practical. According to a website extolling the initiative, "consistent standards will provide appropriate benchmarks for all students, regardless of where they live." The Common Core claims to provide appropriate benchmarks to all students everywhere. Is this in fact the case?

Not for many parents in our school district who are angry that an inspired kindergarten curriculum has been replaced with a banal one.

Our son started kindergarten loving to read and talking with the teacher. He grew to dread the hours he spends listening to prepackaged materials and taking standardized tests. Many of the parents at our elementary school worry that a working system has been broken. Surely there is a way to help underperforming schools raise their standards without us lowering ours.

Is our school an exception? I don't think so. One reason is provided by Alexis de Tocqueville in *Democracy in America*. According to Tocqueville, America's political culture thrives when people participate on every level of government and society. By doing things for ourselves—such as teachers organizing the curriculum or parents assisting with lesson plans—

we become invested and feel satisfaction in the educational and political process. The Common Core makes it easier for schools to use scripted curricula, thereby draining initiative out of the classroom.

Our son used to skip on his way up the entrance to school. This habit stopped shortly after he started the program designed to satisfy the Common Core criteria. We, like many parents around the country, have begun to realize that the rhetoric of the Common Core does not match our children's experience of it—and cannot.

The Common Core Curriculum and Scripted Lesson Plans

My wife and I attended a coffee klatch to discuss the Common Core with our state senator. A teacher stood up and said, with a tremble in her voice and a tear in her eye,

> If parents knew what the Common Core is doing to the classroom, there would be a revolt.

What is happening to the classroom as a result of the Common Core? If you would like an answer to this question, spend some time with the ELA materials on the New York State Education Department (NYSED) website.

On the EngageNY homepage, click on the words "Common Core Curriculum & Assessments." Follow the links until you get to Grade 5 ELA Module 1. Download the 589-page document.

The module is on the Universal Declaration of Human Rights (UDHR). This is a fine topic to discuss in school, though the module does confirm worries that the Common Core could be used to promote a political ideology. My critique here is that this module—despite a disclaimer on the website—is a script, and scripts suck the oxygen out of a classroom.

Here are a few minutes of the script:

Minutes 0–10: The teacher reads the first learning target aloud: "I can follow our class norms when I participate in a conversation." Then, the teacher asks students to provide synonyms of the words *follow* and *participate*. Next, the teacher tells a student to read the learning target: "I can define human rights." For the remainder of the time, students discuss the meaning of the words *human* and *rights* in small groups.

Minutes 11–15: The teacher checks in with students using the Fist to Five protocol. The teacher is told, "Ask students to indicate with their fist if they did not attend to the class norms at all, or five fingers if they attended to all class norms consistently. They can choose to show one to four fingers to indicate that their attention to norms was somewhere in between."

Minutes 16–20: The teacher distributes copies of the UDHR to each student and says, "This is a really cool primary source called the Universal Declaration of Human Rights, sometimes called the UDHR. We will learn more about this document in the next few days. Look it over. What do you notice about the way this document is structured or laid out on this page?" Furthermore, the teacher is instructed, "Do NOT explain the content of the text; simply give students a moment to get oriented and notice how the document is structured."

The script continues with this kind of detail for the rest of the year in a sequence of lessons, units, modules, and assessments. Teachers are not allowed to use their own methods to introduce the material, manage the classroom, or share their own wisdom. Students are not encouraged to connect the material to their own lives, events in the world, or things that may interest them. The script tell the teachers and students, at all times, what to say and do.

The Common Core ELA curriculum does not treat teachers or students with dignity.

Lest you think that teachers can afford to ignore the modules, consider this fact. The Race to the Top program requires states to use value-added modeling in teacher evaluations. In other words, states rank teachers and school districts on how students do on the Common Core tests (the Partnership for Assessment of Readiness for College and Careers [PARCC] and the Smarter Balanced Assessment Consortium [SBAC]). That is why many school districts in New York make teachers use these modules designed to prepare students for these tests. It is also why school districts around the country—including in Connecticut, South Carolina, Louisiana, and Arizona—are using these modules.

The Common Core is creating a national ELA curriculum, one that dedicates more time to subjects like learning targets and the Fist to Five protocol than to classical literature or creative writing. The teacher at the coffee klatch was right. People are revolting against the Common Core as they learn what it does to the classroom.

The Villains

Bill Gates, Bankroller of the Common Core

The multinational software giant Microsoft once bundled its Explorer search engine with Windows and refused, for a time, to have Windows run WordPerfect, a competitor to Microsoft Word. As head of Microsoft, Bill Gates wanted everyone to use the same program. As funder of the Common Core, I believe he wants to do the same with our children.

The Common Core is one of the most effective educational reform movements in U.S. history. Gates is a financial backer of this movement. Looking at this connection enables us to see why the United States should be wary of letting any one person or group acquire too much control over education policy.

Launched in 2009 and now adopted by forty-five states, the Common Core articulates a single set of educational standards in language arts and mathematics. Although the Common Core claims not to tell teachers what or how to teach, school districts must prove to state legislatures or the federal government (via the Race to the Top program) that they are complying with the Common Core. The simplest and most cost-effective way for a school district to do that is to purchase an approved reading or math program.

The Common Core transfers bread-and-butter curriculum decisions from the local to the state and national levels.

On the Common Core website, Gates applauds this development, stating that the initiative brings the nation closer to "supporting effective teaching in every classroom." Here, I believe, one sees a link between Gates's business and advocacy sides.

The Common Core may raise standards in some school districts, but one ought to read the literature with a critical eye. The Common Core has not been field-tested anywhere. The Common Core does not address many root causes of underperforming schools, such as hungry students or dangerous neighborhoods. And the Common Core has an opportunity cost, namely, that it forces thriving school districts to adopt programs that may be a worse fit for the student body.

We can learn a lesson from the recent history of the computing industry. Apple and Microsoft have pressed each other to make better applications, phones, notepads, and cameras. Though Gates may have wanted to vanquish Apple, Steve Jobs prompted him to improve his products, which in turn benefited every computer user. Competition brings out the best in people and institutions. The Common Core standardizes curricula and thereby hinders competition among educational philosophies.

Surely, one could say, certain standards are self-evidently good. A Common Core principle of first grade math is that students should "attend to precision" and "look for and make use of structure." Just as a computer program requires each number, space, and function to be in its right spot to operate, so too the standards emphasize thinking in an orderly fashion and showing each step of the work.

In *Letters to a Young Scientist,* the Harvard biologist E. O. Wilson argues that the demand for precision can hurt the scientific imagination. Wilson celebrates the fanciful nature of innovation by reflecting on how Darwin formulated the idea of descent with modification while sailing on the HMS *Beagle* and Newton discovered that white light is a mix of colored lights while playing with a prism. Though teachers sometimes need to write orderly equations on a blackboard, real progress comes "amid a litter of doodled paper." Doodling is a prelude to a eureka moment, the fuel of scientific research.

Would it be wise to nationalize an educational policy that frowns on doodling?

One could argue about the details of the Common Core standards: how to strike the right balance, say, between fiction and nonfiction, humanities and sciences, doodling and straight lines, and so forth. And yet this approach concedes that America ought to have the same approach in every classroom.

America needs many kinds of excellent programs and schools: International Baccalaureate programs, science and technology schools, Montessori schools, religious schools, vocational schools, bilingual schools, outdoor schools, and good public schools. Even within programs and schools, teachers should be encouraged to teach their passions and areas of expertise. Teachers inspire lifelong learning by bringing a class to a nature center, replicating an experiment from *Popular Science,* taking a field trip to the state or national capital, or assigning a favorite novel. A human being is not a computer, and a good education is not formatted in a linear code.

As a result of the Common Core, teachers in our school district must now open boxes filled with reading materials, workbooks, and tests from a "learning company." How depressing and unnecessary. As Apple and Google have shown, great work can be done when talented employees are granted power and encouraged to innovate.

In regard to education policy, I'd prefer Bill Gates to have a loud voice in his school district but a quieter one in mine.

David Coleman, Architect of the Common Core

In summer 2008, David Coleman changed the course of American education. For decades, reformers had argued that the country needed a national standards-based model of education to ensure economic prosperity. He helped make that a reality by convincing Bill Gates to support the Common Core State Standards Initiative, to the tune of more than $200 million.

In part because of his experience supervising the writing of the standards, Coleman became the head of the College Board, where his philosophy of education shapes how U.S. high schools prepare students for college.

He has expressed this vision in an essay published by the College Board, "Cultivating Wonder." With this document and the results of the Common Core, it's easy to see where his grand plans fall short.

In "Cultivating Wonder," Coleman unpacks several Common Core standards, shows how students may decipher classic works of literature, and reflects on appropriate questions to ask students, revealing the philosophy of the Common Core and the College Board.

As a professor of political philosophy, I agree that education ought to cultivate wonder. The first book of political philosophy, Plato's *Republic,* begins with Socrates experiencing wonder at a remark made by one of his interlocutors. Wonder is what compels us to keep investigating a question using every resource at our disposal.

Yet Coleman's pedagogical vision stifles this kind of wonder by imposing tight restrictions on what may be thought—or at least what may be expressed to earn teacher approval, high grades, and good test scores. He expects students to answer questions merely by stringing together key words in the text before them.

This does not teach philosophy or thinking; it teaches the practice of rote procedures, conformity, and obedience.

The first standard is the foundation of his vision. "Read closely to determine what the text says explicitly and to make logical inferences from it," it reads, and "cite specific textual evidence when writing or speaking to support conclusions drawn from the text." According to Coleman, the first standard teaches a rigorous, deductive approach to reading that compels students to extract as much information from the text as possible.

Throughout the document, he reiterates that students need to identify key words in a text. He analyzes passages from *Hamlet, The Adventures of Huckleberry Finn,* the Gettysburg Address, and an essay by Martha Graham. There is minimal discussion of historical context or outside sources that may make the material come alive. For instance, he suggests that teachers ask students, "What word does Lincoln use most often in the address?" rather than, say, discuss the Civil War. In fact, he disparages this approach. "Great questions make the text the star of the classroom; the most powerful evidence and insight for answering lies within the text or texts being read. Most good questions are text dependent and text specific."

As a professor, of course I demand that my students provide evidence to support their arguments. Coleman's pedagogical vision, however, does not prepare students for college. He discourages students from making connections between ideas, texts, or events in the world—in a word, from thinking. Students are not encouraged to construct knowledge and understanding; they must simply be adept at repeating it.

His philosophy of education transfers across disciplines. After analyzing literary passages, he observes, "Similar work could be done for texts . . . in other areas such as social studies, history, science and technical subjects." Like a chef's signature flavor, Coleman's philosophy of education permeates the myriad programs that the College Board runs.

Computers can grade the responses generated from his philosophy of education. Students read a passage and then answer questions using terms from it, regardless of whether the text is about history, literature, physics, or U.S. history. The U.S. Postal Service sorts letters using handwriting-recognition technology, and with a little tinkering, this kind of software could be used to score the SAT or Advanced Placement (AP) exams.

Coleman's vision will end up harming the U.S. economy and our democratic culture.

The United States should be wary of emulating countries that use a standards-based model of education. In *World Class Learners,* the scholar Yong Zhao commends America's tradition of local control of the schools and an educational culture that encourages sports, the arts, internships, and other extracurricular pursuits. In diverse ways, U.S. schools have educated many successful intellectuals, artists, and inventors. By contrast, the Chinese model of education emphasizes rigorous standards and high-stakes tests, preeminently the *gaokao* college entrance exam. Chinese policy makers rue, however, how this education culture stifles creativity, curiosity, and entrepreneurship. The Common Core will lead us to the same trap. Educators should not discard what has made the United States a hotbed of innovation and entrepreneurship.

Democracy depends on citizens treating one another with respect. In perhaps his most famous public statement, Coleman told a room of educators not to teach students to write personal narratives, because "as you grow up in this world, you realize that people really don't give a shit about what you feel or what you think." This statement expresses, albeit more crassly, the same sentiment as his essay on cultivating wonder. He demands that students do what they are told and not offer their own perspectives on things. Ideally in a democracy, by contrast, citizens have a sincere interest in what other citizens have to say. As John Dewey argued in *Democracy and Education,* the purpose of the schools is to create a democratic culture, not one that replicates the worst features of the market economy.

A recurrent defense of the Common Core is that the standards are good but the implementation has been bad. Even if Coleman's educational vision is perfectly actualized, it is still profoundly flawed. Under Common Core, from the time they enter kindergarten to the time they graduate from high school, students will have few opportunities to ask their own questions or come up with their own ideas. It's time for Americans to find alternatives to Coleman's educational vision.

Michael Barber, Pearson Deliverologist

Who stands to gain from education reforms such as the controversial Common Core standards?

One big winner is the British publishing company Pearson, which delivered 9 million high-stakes tests to students across the United States in 2014, including the PARCC Common Core assessments. Pearson has an especially tight hold on New York's education system, which one critic has compared to the grip of an octopus. Pearson runs the edTPA program, which certifies New York teachers, and the company has a $32 million contract to administer the state's end-of-year tests. And it offers a wide variety of services to implement the Common Core, including curriculum models and tools to measure student understanding.

The company is expanding its brand into the United Kingdom, Australia, Italy, South Africa, Brazil, India, and Saudi Arabia. Pearson earns more than $8 billion in annual global sales, with much more to come if countries continue to use standardized tests to rate students, teachers, and schools.

We can learn more about Pearson and its sweeping vision for the future by turning to a book by the company's chief academic officer, Michael Barber. In *Deliverology 101: A Field Guide for Educational Leaders,* he lays out his philosophy and, unintentionally, reveals why parents, teachers, and politicians must do everything they can to break Pearson's stranglehold on education policy around the world.

Barber has worked on education policy for British prime minister Tony Blair as well as for McKinsey and Company. *Deliverology,* written with assistance from two other McKinsey experts, is clearly inflected by the worldview of management consulting.

The authors define *deliverology* as "the emerging science of getting things done" and "a systematic process for driving progress and delivering results in government and the public sector." The book targets systems leaders, politicians who support education reform, and delivery leaders, employees responsible for the day-to-day implementation of structural change.

Deliverology alternates between painting a big picture of what needs to be done and offering maxims such as "To aspire means to lead from the front" and "Endless public debate will create problems that could potentially derail your delivery effort."

Pearson just happens to be one of the world's largest vendors of the products Barber recommends for building education systems.

Barber believes in the "alchemy of relationships," or the power of a small group of people working together to enact structural change. For example, Barber applauds Barack Obama's Race to the Top program for providing a "once-in-a-generation opportunity to transform public education in America," including through the Common Core. Barber's book offers leaders advice on how to implement the Common Core standards that Pearson employees helped write.

Taking inspiration from Margaret Thatcher's motto "Don't tell me what, tell me how," Barber rarely discusses what schools should teach or cites scholarship on pedagogy. Instead, the book emphasizes again and again that leaders need metrics—for example, standardized test scores—to measure whether reforms are helping children become literate and numerate.

This spring, a prominent anti–Common Core activist tweeted, "I don't think the Ed reformers understand the sheer fury of marginalized parents." Barber understands this fury but thinks the "laggards" will come around once enough people see the positive results.

Deliverology even instructs leaders how to respond to common excuses from people who object to education reform.

COMMON EXCUSES	RESPONSE
The changes you're asking for will have unintended consequences.	We will have mechanisms for ensuring potential consequences aren't realized (e.g., monitoring indicators of unintended consequences).
The changes you're asking for are risky.	The risks of inaction are greater.
The target is wrong.	The changes were chosen from fact-based analysis and make sense when viewed as part of the trajectory.

Deliverology is a field guide—or a battle plan—showing education reformers how to push ahead through all resistance and never have second thoughts. As Barber quotes Robert F. Kennedy, "only those who dare to fail greatly can ever achieve greatly." Parents and teachers who do not want to adapt to the new state of affairs are branded "defenders of the status quo." Barber ends the book by telling reformers to stick with their plans but acknowledge the emotional argument of opponents: "I understand why you might be angry; I would not enjoy this if it were happening to me either."

But Pearson's investment in the Common Core has become a lightning rod for criticism. Professor Nancy Carlsson-Paige of Lesley University contributed to a report identifying problems with the Common Core standards, including the one that requires kindergartners to "read emergent texts with purpose and understanding." According to the report, there is no scholarly basis for setting this bar for kindergartners. In fact, the evidence suggests, expecting children to read too early can have adverse consequences. Early-childhood researchers have shown the benefits of play-based kindergarten for cognitive, social, emotional, and physical development. "Children learn through playful, hands-on experiences with materials, the natural world and engaging, caring adults." The report calls for the Common Core kindergarten standards to be withdrawn.

Politicians are listening to informed dissent against the Common Core and its corporate sponsors. In New York, state senator Terry Gipson (D-Rhinebeck) introduced legislation to sever the state's connections to Pearson. After identifying problems with the company's Common Core exams, Gipson said, "This is a for-profit corporation funded with taxpayer money, so we have more than enough reason to ask the state Education Department to cease and desist all relations."

Expect such resistance to grow—and for good reason. Parents, educators, and politicians no longer buy what Pearson is selling.

How Democratic Party Elites Educate Their Own Kids

For years, U.S. secretary of education Arne Duncan's children attended public school in Virginia. Now, they go to the University of Chicago Laboratory School, the private school where Chicago mayor Rahm Emanuel sends his kids and where

Barack Obama sent his daughters when he lived in Chicago. The annual tuition is approximately $30,000.

During the Common Core rollout, New York education commissioner John King sent his daughters to a private Montessori school near Albany; New York governor Andrew Cuomo's daughters, on their part, attended an elite boarding school in Massachusetts.

There is nothing wrong with private school. The problem here, though, is that too many Democratic elites advocate education reforms, such as the Common Core standards, charter schools, and high-stakes testing, with minimal firsthand knowledge of how the reforms affect schools or children. In sending their children to private schools, Democratic elites exempt themselves from policies that they might oppose if they saw their own children being harmed by them.

In 2008, many Democrats hoped that Barack Obama would send his children to public school as Jimmy Carter did before him. In their book *President Obama and Education Reform,* Robert Maranto and Michael Q. McShane explain why that was not likely to happen.

The key to understanding Obama's education policy, according to Maranto and McShane, is his biography. Obama attended the prestigious Punahou School in Hawaii, an experience that prepared him for college and law school. Obama also observed from a distance a Hawaiian public school system rife with ethnic violence, low academic standards, and an unresponsive bureaucracy. These experiences influenced Obama's decision to send his daughters to Sidwell Friends, the elite Washington, D.C., institution whose alumni include the younger Albert Gore and Chelsea Clinton.

As president, Obama advocated reforms to the public education system that include upping merit pay, weakening tenure rules, and evaluating teachers by student test scores. Obama's most controversial education policy, however, was the Race to the Top program that gave states additional incentives to adopt the Common Core standards.

The Common Core, according to one critic, is "the product of a push by private foundations acting in the interest of multinational corporations to colonize public education in the United States." The U.S. Chamber of Commerce, the Business Roundtable, and corporations such as IBM and Exxon have backed the Common Core. Still, politicians are essential to generate sufficient support for effective market-based education reform.

Maranto and McShane applaud Obama's efforts to recast education reform in the language of equity, justice, and civil rights. Just as President Richard Nixon was able to convince Republicans to make peace with China, Obama has been able to convince Democrats to support market-based education reforms.

The question remains, though: are these reforms making public schools better? Or are they widening the gap between the kinds of education offered at public and elite private schools?

According to education scholar Diane Ravitch, most educated parents believe that good schools have full curricula, experienced staffs, arts programs, well-staffed libraries, beautiful campuses, and small classes. All of these things are par for the course at America's finest private schools.

But it costs a lot of money to offer students this kind of education. In response, education reformers favor economies of scale, where students across the country take the same standardized tests, as well as reforms that tend to favor corporations rather than teachers. For example, the Race to the Top program awarded Pearson almost $200 million to develop the PARCC Common Core tests.

However, many parents resent the way in which children's education now consists of little more than preparing for and taking standardized tests. One blogger in Chicago, for example, notes that the Lab School offers a rich arts curriculum, small classes, a unionized workforce, and a policy of not giving students a standardized test until they are at least 14 years old. Meanwhile, children in the local public schools must take a steady stream of standardized tests and have little exposure to history, science, art, or music. The blogger wryly observes that Arne Duncan has chosen for his own children a school that has been minimally affected by the reforms that he advocated as education secretary.

Since at least the 1990s, education reformers have argued that schools should be run like businesses focused on the bottom line—in this case, test scores. Parents and educators from across the spectrum reply that our society should strive to offer all children the kind of opportunities provided at the finest private schools.

Unfortunately, too many Democratic elites have joined the side of market-based economic reform. They may do so with a clear conscience, perhaps, because their own children do not suffer the consequences.

How Obama and Congress Cemented the Common Core

The country's main education law is the Every Student Succeeds Act (ESSA). ESSA authorizes the federal government to provide funds to states if they agree to certain conditions. ESSA is a reauthorization of the Elementary and Secondary Education Act of 1965 and one of the signature achievements of the Obama administration.[1]

1. Later in the book, I dispute U.S. secretary of education Betsy DeVos's claim that the Common Core is dead at the federal level. The ESSA framework remains firmly in place during the Trump administration.

ESSA states that the secretary of education "shall not attempt to influence, incentivize or coerce" states to adopt the controversial Common Core education standards in math and ELA and that the federal government should not determine how much student test scores factor into teacher evaluations. It would appear that the era of high-stakes Common Core testing has ended.

Unfortunately, Congress remains firmly committed to test-based education reform. The Every Student Succeeds Act and Obama's Testing Action Plan simply offer new ways to force states to administer tests that have sparked a rebellion among parents and educators across the country against overtesting and the narrowing of the curriculum to test subjects.

In a press statement, the Department of Education offered an apology, of sorts, for the "unnecessary testing" that is "consuming too much instructional time and creating undue stress for educators and students." Senator Lamar Alexander (R-Tenn.) said that the Every Student Succeeds Act is "the most significant step towards local control in 25 years."

Yet ESSA, according to Senator Patty Murray (D-Wash.), includes "strong federal guardrails to ensure all students have access to a quality education." As it turns out, these guardrails provide as much freedom to the states as a passenger has on a roller coaster.

The states have to continue the testing regimen established with the No Child Left Behind Act under President George W. Bush, administering math and English language assessments to students in grades 3 through 8 and once in high school.

In fact, the ESSA requires states to test an even larger percentage of students than under No Child Left Behind. Under ESSA, states would be permitted to provide alternate assessments to no more than 1 percent of the students on the grounds that they possess "significant cognitive disabilities." Consequently, a much higher percentage of students in special education have to take the tests. The law also increases the pressure on states to administer tests and use English language learners' and minorities' test scores for accountability purposes.

The law technically allows states to create their own provisions for students who opt out of tests, but it also requires states to measure at least 95 percent of all students annually. Students could refuse to take the tests, but if enough of them do, then their state would risk losing federal education aid. According to education scholar Mercedes Schneider, "the federal government is trying to force the testing without taking responsibility for forcing the testing."

How can people say that ESSA is a U-turn from the education policies of the recent past? Under ESSA, the federal government may not tell states what academic standards to adopt or how student test scores should be used in teacher evaluations. Nonetheless, states have to submit accountability plans to the Department of Education for approval, and these accountability plans have to weigh test scores more than any other factor. Furthermore, under the act, states have to use "evidence-based interventions" in the bottom 5 percent of schools, determined, again, by test scores.

In short, states are free to choose test-based accountability policies approved by the secretary of education or lose access to federal Title I funds that sustain schools in low-income communities across the country. In a move that belies Alexander's claim about local control, the Department of Education provides "office hours" for states or districts that wish to meet its "policy objectives and requirements under the law."

Does the law at least permit states to escape the Common Core? It is hard to see how. According to ESSA, each state has to adopt "challenging state academic standards." The Obama administration's Testing Action Plan stipulates that assessment systems should measure student knowledge and skills against "state-developed college- and career-ready standards"—which has long been code for the Common Core. So, yes, states could invest hundreds of millions of dollars into writing new academic standards and making aligned tests, but there is no guarantee that the secretary of education would approve the standards or tests.

Advocates of high-stakes Common Core testing have applauded ESSA. Catherine Brown, the director of education policy at the Center for American Progress, said the law "appears to allow the department to set parameters in key areas and enforce statutory requirements." John Engler of the Business Roundtable likewise applauded the law for keeping test scores "a central feature" of state accountability systems. Lanea Erickson at Third Way praised the law for throwing "some much-needed water on the political firestorm around testing."

These advocates have not changed their minds about the Common Core or testing. They are just happy to shift the responsibility for administering it to the states rather than the federal government if that would help defuse parent and educator animosity. They misunderstand the justified anger that fuels the test-refusal movement.

Parents are in an uproar about the Common Core not because they have been brainwashed by the unions or want school to be easy for their children. Rather, they object to federal education policies that have narrowed the curriculum to standardized test prep in two academic subjects or, more precisely, peculiar interpretations of math and ELA. Until that changes, parents of all backgrounds and means will still clamor for the same kind of education that wealthy, connected people demand for their children.

The Standards Themselves

> It is this duality of myself with myself that makes thinking
> a true activity, in which I am both the one who asks and the
> one who answers.
>
> —HANNAH ARENDT, *The Life of the Mind*

The English Language Arts Standards Stifle Thought

How can teachers encourage thinking in school?

Arendt's *The Life of the Mind* influences my answer. As an educator, my job is to prompt students to think—or, in her terms, to have soundless dialogues within themselves. One way to accomplish that is to structure courses as a conversation between philosophers. In my American political thought course, for instance, I teach lessons on the liberal John Rawls and the conservative Leo Strauss. An integral part of that particular unit is for students to enact a conversation between those two figures in their own minds.

Ideally, when students leave my courses, they will be able to hear different viewpoints speak up in their heads whenever they themselves consider, say, America's role in the world or the just distribution of resources in a society. My goal is not to indoctrinate but to render students more thoughtful, more broad-minded, which means being able to look at political things from multiple angles. To address the most pressing problems of our day, we need our upcoming generations to become more thoughtful.

This brings me to a raging debate in American politics about the purpose of education. Let me describe the position that I oppose. The Common Core State Standards initiative aims to prepare all American children for success in college and careers in the twenty-first century. For too long, children in poverty or remote locations have not had access to a strong curriculum. The Common Core seeks to offset that trend by setting a bar in literacy and numeracy, one that states, schools, teachers, and students can reach in different ways.

The Common Core emphasizes the skill of close reading. What follows now is a definition of that skill as provided by PARCC, a consortium responsible for Common Core assessment:

> Close, analytic reading stresses engaging with a text of sufficient complexity directly and examining meaning thoroughly and methodically, encouraging students to read and reread deliberately. Directing student attention on the text itself empowers students to understand the central ideas and key supporting details.

The purpose of the Common Core is to teach students to answer questions using evidence from texts, a useful skill for education at all levels as well as at nearly any job. According to polls, people tend to approve of the Common Core when introduced to it at this level of generality.

Problems become apparent, however, in the program's actual implementation. Common Core assignments and tests require students to read a passage and then submit answers using exact words from the text, a pedagogy that facilitates computer grading. Students under Common Core do poorly if they answer questions using material that is not in the assigned passages. Put in Kantian terms, schools now train determinate judgment—the placing of round pegs in round holes—rather than reflective judgment, the crafting of singular responses to complex problems.

From an Arendtian perspective, the Common Core is a misguided response to the crisis in education. Students across the country now read so-called informational texts written by anonymous scribes at educational corporations such as Pearson or McGraw-Hill. The Common Core pressures schools to use a banal curriculum and pedagogy. Should students know how to use evidence to answer a question? Of course. Should that be the almost exclusive focus of the curriculum? No, not if we want schools to encourage students to connect ideas across texts or to confront pressing problems in the world.

Arendt's concept of natality may give us two clues as to how we can get out of this situation. One is to value the power of educators and citizens to choose, or create, educational possibilities. Throughout her work, Arendt criticizes the thoughtless exercise of technocratic power. She goes on to call on people to act together on matters of public concern. Fortunately, America has a tradition of locally controlled schools, so an Arendtian might argue that school boards, for instance, should remain a site of political debate and decision.

Furthermore, an Arendtian might argue that schools should encourage children to think for themselves and practice disclosing themselves with one another. In her essay "The Crisis in Education" (1954), Arendt contests the child-centered focus of progressive education. Though she is correct that schools have the responsibility of conserving the achievements of the past and passing them on to the next generation, I think that she misinterprets John Dewey's philosophy of education. Dewey's thesis in *Democracy and Education* is that schools should make material interesting, not easy or fun, but rather tap into a student's care for the world. An Arendtian would appreciate this impulse, particularly when the present alternative is a monotonous routine of finding key words in short texts.

Schools should provide the soil in which a child's propensity to think can grow and blossom. In this particular moment, that principle requires political actors to oppose the Common Core and envision educational alternatives.

The Math Standards Do Not Prepare Children for STEM Majors or Careers

I am reading a second-grade math homework assignment. To get full credit, students must not only determine which of two numbers is higher; they must also demonstrate knowledge of place value. The assignment illustrates Common Core State Standard 2.0A.A.1:

> Use addition and subtraction within 100 to solve one- and two-step word problems involving situations of adding to, taking from, putting together, taking apart, and comparing, with unknowns in all positions, e.g., by using drawings and equations with a symbol for the unknown number to represent the problem.

In case this is opaque to you, NYSED offers the following explanation:

> Real-life situations provide context and empirical support for the mathematical properties of addition (commutativity and associativity, which combine to make the so-called "any which way rule") and for the mathematical relationship between addition and subtraction (subtraction is an unknown-addend problem).

Although I studied statistics and econometrics in graduate school, I must admit that I can barely follow these quotes. Later in the NYSED document, we encounter the following statement:

> The Common Core State Standards present a balanced approach to mathematics that stresses equally the goals of conceptual understanding, fluency, and application.

On the contrary, this statement is crystal clear. The standards teach good things, for example, conceptual understanding. If you don't understand the Common Core, the implication is that it's your problem.

George Orwell warned against this kind of abuse of language in his essay "Politics and the English Language." Orwell argued that authors should write as clearly and simply as the material allows. He criticized authors who use "pretentious diction" to give "an air of scientific impartiality to biased judgments." Authors can use big words and convoluted sentences to make readers feel stupid. In this case, the Common Core literature may intimidate administrators, teachers, and parents to accept the new educational regime.

Parents of young children *might* be willing to endorse the Common Core math standards if they are confident that the payoff will be worth it. In a policy paper called "Can This Country Survive Common Core's College Readiness Level?," two professors on the Common Core Validation Committee, R. James Milgram and Sandra Stotsky, observe that the math progression does not reach precalculus. College students who did not take a precalculus course in high school rarely go on to earn a bachelor's degree in a STEM area. In point of fact, the Common Core does not prepare many students for careers in science, mathematics, engineering, finance, or economics. "At this time, we can only conclude that a gigantic fraud has been perpetrated on this country, in particular on parents in this country, by those developing, promoting, or endorsing Common Core's standards."

When discussing politics, citizens should speak to one another as clearly and sincerely as possible. Right now, the Common Core literature uses technical terms and tortuous prose to sell an educational philosophy that may not deliver what it promises.

The Next Generation Science Standards Lead to Computer Simulations, Not Hands-On Tasks

The state Board of Regents has approved the New York State P–12 Science Learning Standards. The standards identify the practices and ideas children will study in science class from kindergarten until high school graduation. The new standards are based on the national Next Generation Science Standards and claim to teach children science, technology, engineering, and math. According to state education commissioner MaryEllen Elia, these standards will "provide equitable learning opportunities" so that all students will be ready for college and careers.

Unfortunately, the new science standards are created by the same group that produced the Common Core standards, are aligned to the Common Core standards, and are designed for high-stakes online testing. The Regents could have blazed a new path for science education in the country; instead, the Regents continue to build an education system that parents abhor.

Achieve is a Washington, D.C., based organization that developed the Next Generation Science Standards as well as the Common Core State Standards in math and ELA. Achieve's contributors include the Bill and Melinda Gates Foundation, Chevron, DuPont, and ExxonMobil. ExxonMobil CEO Rex Tillerson once explained why he supports education reform: "I'm not sure public schools understand that we're their customer—that we, the business community, are your customer." For Tillerson, corporations have entered the standards debate because they want a better "product," not because they care about democracy or protecting the environment.

It is a shame that the Regents trusted and relied on Achieve and its funders, such as ExxonMobil, to structure science education in New York.

The new standards explicitly align with the Common Core. Here, for example, is a prekindergarten performance expectation for physical sciences: "Ask questions and use observations to test the claim that different kinds of matter exist as either solid or liquid." This standard connects with the Common Core ELA prekindergarten standard for reading informational text: "With prompting and support, ask and answer questions about details in a text." While many early-childhood researchers and practitioners recognize that young children learn about the world by playing with blocks, water, sand, and dirt, these science standards demand that kids read at an age-inappropriate level.

The new standards share the Common Core's focus on "close reading." There are occasions in life when one needs to provide exact evidence from a text. But close reading provides few opportunities for children to formulate their own hypotheses or proceed in an unconventional manner. Even if you agree with the content of the science standards, one may still protest indoctrinating students into providing the one correct answer. That is not how scientists think or how good private schools teach science.

To understand what is on the horizon for testing, one should read the National Research Council's *A Framework for K–12 Science Education*. The book explains that science education requires the alignment of curriculum, instruction, teacher development, and assessment and promotes the development of computer-based assessments. The framework dismisses the idea that standards should emphasize visits from experts to the classroom, field trips to science centers and aquariums, or experiential learning. Administering and scoring hands-on tasks "can be cumbersome and expensive"; whereas "computer-based assessment offers a promising alternative."

Given that the federal Every Student Succeeds Act requires testing of science in the grade spans 3–5, 6–9, and 10–12, one may soon see online science testing in New York. And given how testing drives the curriculum, one may anticipate science instruction to be done increasingly on computers. Some have said that science class will become more "hands-on" with the new standards. That is absurd. Clicking a mouse on online science assessments does not constitute hands-on science, nor does it generate wonder at the natural world. The clear beneficiaries of this adoption are testing and tutoring companies.

To be fair, the new standards include material that students should know about science. For some students, the new standards and aligned curricula and testing may constitute an improvement in science education. But the choice does not have to be between the Achieve package of science education or nothing. New York has some of the world's best scientists, professors, and researchers. Why are we using a set of science standards developed by a Washington, D.C., group funded by oil companies?

When historians look back on this era, they will see Achieve and its funders waging a battle against parents who do not want education to be about preparing for online tests. New Yorkers should tell the Regents that they made a mistake adopting Achieve's science standards and that we need to plan an exit strategy.

The College Board's Interest in Advanced Placement U.S. History

In fall 2014, teachers and students in Colorado demanded a say in how history is taught in the state's public schools. The protests erupted in response to a proposal by the Jefferson County School Board to revise the APUSH curriculum framework to emphasize patriotism, the free market, and respect for authority. The teachers and students replied that this account of history whitewashes injustice and the importance of civil disobedience.

But the Colorado protesters and their sympathizers across the country may have done more harm than good by cementing the College Board's virtual monopoly on how U.S. history is taught to college-bound students.

The controversy started when the College Board, which administers the AP exams that high school students nationwide take at the end of each school year, released a draft of its new APUSH framework. This provoked a backlash among conservatives unhappy about what they saw as a too-negative assessment of the founding of the United States, among other things. Subsequently, the College Board released a revised draft, and the Jefferson County School Board responded with its proposal, which sparked the student–teacher protests.

The national media have by and large presented this story as a clash between the forces of reaction and the forces of progress, between provincial conservatives and scholars who acknowledge the role of women and minorities in U.S. history. While this narrative contains a grain of truth, it overlooks the question of who should decide what version of history should be taught in schools.

My concern is with the College Board's attempt to foreclose debate about how communities teach history to college-bound high school students. It is not the details of the APUSH curricular framework that worry me but a private company's push to usurp curricular decisions from locally elected school boards. What the dispute is really about, then, is democratic control of schools.

In *The Human Condition,* the German political philosopher Hannah Arendt argues that storytellers, or historians, play a vital role in the community by determining what is remembered or forgotten about political events. Historians not only recount what happened; they also signal to the community what kinds of events are worth celebrating or not. For Arendt, one of the central tasks of politics—what she calls the vita activa—is fostering debate about the stories a community tells about itself.

At the time, the College Board said that it supported the students' protest against an attempt "to censor aspects of the AP U.S. history course." That is one way to frame the debate; another is that the College Board wants to prohibit local school boards from revising its product or contesting its version of U.S. history.

Of course, there are elements in the APUSH curriculum framework that may be as good as or better than what the Jefferson County School Board would choose. But that is not a reason to prohibit school boards from having a say in the U.S. history curriculum. In *Federalist* 51, James Madison wrote, "Ambition must be made to counteract ambition." If men were angels, there would be no need for checks and balances, but because humans tend to favor people who agree with them, it is necessary to distribute power widely throughout society. In this case, the ambition of the Jefferson County School Board counteracts the ambition of the College Board. No one person or group should hold a monopoly on something as valuable as how a community remembers its past or envisions its future.

Here is a thought experiment for people who still favor the revised APUSH curriculum framework over the Jefferson County School Board's alternative: if Julie Williams, the outspoken member of the Jefferson County School Board behind the revision proposal, became president of the College Board, how much power would you want her to have? This consideration may help us gain appreciation for Arendt's and Madison's arguments for why communities should have the ongoing power to determine what history they will teach their young people.

Core Knowledge Cannot Salvage the Common Core

Can the Common Core be saved? Can its focus on close-reading skills be supplemented by a content-rich curriculum? Can the Common Core's role in promoting national standardized tests still lead to a more culturally literate population? E. D. Hirsch Jr. answers yes to all of these questions in his book *Why Knowledge Matters: Rescuing Our Children from Failed Education Theories.*

Hirsch, a professor emeritus of education and humanities at the University of Virginia, published a best-selling book in the 1980s called *Cultural Literacy: What Every American Needs to Know.* In it, he included a list of dates, names, events, and so forth that cultured Americans already know and that, for egalitarian reasons, should be taught to all young people in public schools.

The Common Core is a set of standards and not a curriculum. Though the Common Core has appendixes that have recommended readings, the Common Core emphasizes above all the skill of close reading, expressed by the first anchor standard that students must "read closely to determine what the text says explicitly and to make logical inferences from it."

Hirsch wrote blogs for the *Huffington Post* in 2013 supporting the Common Core. In *Why Knowledge Matters,* Hirsch is surprisingly blunt in his critique of it. "These empty standards were created out of political expediency. The makers of standards and tests have built up an artificial construct ... based on a faulty and unproductive picture of reading comprehension." Hirsch cites research showing that students understand a text better when they focus on its meaning rather than the words themselves. "Paying close attention to the text itself debases comprehension by usurping limited mental resources that would be better applied to pondering the substantive implications and the validity of what the text is saying."

According to Hirsch, "this close-reading standard in the Common Core should be recast (or excised) to conform with the scientific finding that paying attention to word features is less effective than reading for meaning." This is akin to arguing that the Common Core should have a different philosophy of education. And given that the close-reading standard is embedded in the Next Generation Science Standards, the College, Career, and Civic Life (C3) Framework for Social Studies, and the College Board's AP program, Hirsch's demand may be even more revolutionary than he realizes.

Rather than oppose the Common Core, however, Hirsch presents himself as helping it realize its promise. The official document says that standards must be "complemented by a well-developed, content-rich curriculum." So far, test and curriculum makers have tended to ignore the Common Core's admonition to supplement the skill standards with a knowledge-based curriculum.

In the short term, Hirsch would like to see districts and states teach more content-rich curricula, including, but not inclusively, the Core Knowledge program based upon his work. In the longer term, Hirsch would like to see a "nationwide elementary content core."

Is this at all feasible? In 2014, *Politico* ran an article arguing that Common Core architect David Coleman shared the same basic pedagogical outlook as Hirsch. This seems wrong. In 1999, Coleman launched the Grow Network, a company that produced reports to help school districts analyze standardized test scores. In 2008, Coleman met with Bill and Melinda Gates, and they supported his plans to write the Common Core standards. Presently, Coleman leads the College Board, the organization responsible for administering the SAT and AP exams. For his entire professional career, Coleman has been involved in building the current standardized testing industry. To think that he wants to disrupt this industry is to dream of a leopard changing its spots.

In *Why Knowledge Matters,* Hirsch expresses his faith in a national education system that makes all young people culturally literate. "What makes an American competent—whether in Kittery, Maine, or Cleveland, Ohio, or Oakland, California— is mastery of the national dimension of our public sphere. . . . Helping the public to recognize that communal purpose is the practical key to making the Common Core Standards, or any standards, work." In practice, the Common Core has led to the exact kind of education that Hirsch opposes: one based on teaching generic skills rather than rich content. However, Hirsch still holds out hope that someday, somehow, someone one will realize the Common Core's "communal purpose." There are grounds to be skeptical.

On February 2018, *Chalkbeat* published an article on the Gates Foundation's plans to shape the curriculum that schools use across the country. The foundation will fund rating systems to help decision makers select "high-quality" curricular materials. The rating systems will determine whether curricula are aligned to states' education standards—for all intents and purposes, the Common Core. The Gates Foundation has never given a grant to Core Knowledge and has consistently advocated the kinds of standards and tests that Hirsch critiques. The leaders of the Common Core movement may decide that Core Knowledge doesn't fit within their plans.

In *Why Knowledge Matters,* Hirsch continues a decades-long feud with John Dewey (1859–1952) and the progressive education movement in general. According to Hirsch, Dewey embraced certain Romantic themes in his writings on education, including a "providential individualism" that maintains that "the natural growth of a child is an instance of God unfolding His purposes in the world." Though Dewey eventually dropped this kind of religious language, he still believed that educators needed to let children grow naturally. In response, Hirsch maintains, "education is inherently an induction into the adult tribe—and so it has been from the dawn of human social groups. The idea that education is a natural growth has had a relatively recent birth. One hopes it will grow old and die."

Hirsch and his supporters, perhaps because they continue to endorse the ideal of national content standards, have not joined forces with education progressives to oppose the Common Core. Fortunately, some education traditionalists think that such alliances are possible. Here, I would like to give the last word to Jane Robbins, who criticizes the plans for curricular reform in an article for *The American Spectator* called "Bill Gates Doesn't Get It" (June 7, 2018):

> "Quality" in curricula is a nebulous concept. Materials that require students to engage in projects and collaboration, with a healthy dose of social-emotional play-acting, may be considered high-quality in some areas. . . . In others, materials that focus on direct instruction in genuine academic content would win the competition. Local communities are different. So local curricula should be different.

The Global Dimension

The United Nations's Problematic Education Agenda

From its inception in 1945, the UN has been involved with education on a global scale. The UN views education as crucial to eradicating poverty, building peace, and fostering intercultural dialogue, and it remains committed to "a holistic and humanistic vision of quality education worldwide."

Yet there has been a dramatic shift in the UN's educational mission from supporting a well-rounded, humanistic conception of education to one that focuses on teaching children the "hard skills" necessary to participate in the global economy. This turn began with the Millennium Development Goals (2000–2015) and has intensified with the Sustainable Development Goals. One target, for instance, is to "increase the number of youth and adults who have relevant skills, including technical and vocational skills, for employment, decent jobs and entrepreneurship" by 2030.

The UN has thrown its weight behind what Finnish scholar Pasi Sahlberg calls the global education reform movement (GERM). According to Sahlberg, there is a "global unified agenda" to rebuild educational systems to benefit multinational corporations. GERM began in the United States and United Kingdom, and has spread throughout the world. GERM is committed to educational standardization, a focus on literacy and numeracy, high-stakes testing, and centralized control of the schools.

According to Sahlberg, this movement "limits the role of national policy development" and "paralyzes teachers' and schools' attempts to learn from the past and also to learn from each other." In other words, GERM disempowers communities and educators and forces them to teach a narrow set of skills measured by standardized tests.

The UN's sustainable development goals articulate many admirable ideals, including eradicating poverty, combating HIV/AIDS, reducing inequality, and ensuring environmental sustainability. According to Sahlberg, preparing students to tackle global problems requires encouraging creativity and experimentation among schools and teachers. While several recent UN reports mention teaching critical thinking and protecting human rights, the focus is on helping multinational corporations control, for their own benefit, education systems around the globe. For those who think that this is a problem, the time to protest is now.

In fall 2015, Facebook CEO Mark Zuckerberg spoke about the Sustainable Development Goals at the UN Private Sector Forum. He supports the UN's goal of universal Internet access because it creates new jobs, lifts people out of poverty, and gives millions of children "access to affordable learning tools." For Zuckerberg, there is a confluence between the UN's education agenda and Facebook's development of personalized learning platforms.

The UN maintains that the business community should view the UN's education agenda as a chance to pilot technologies, enter markets, train workers, and increase profits. Then UN secretary-general Ban Ki-moon made this pitch in a report titled *The Smartest Investment: A Framework for Business Engagement in Education*. According to Ban, the business world needs a "skilled, innovative workforce" and "investing in education creates a generation of skilled people who will have rising incomes and demands for products and services." The UN promises to help corporations "think about how their business policies and practices can impact education priorities."

First, the report advises business leaders to convince peers to commit to education reform. The report mentions building sustainable societies and saving lives, but the main theme is that the UN's education agenda promotes economic growth and expands business opportunities for companies. For instance, corporations may want to work with the UN because "consumers have indicated a willingness to buy—and reward— socially conscious brands."

Next, according to the report, corporations may improve education by funding organizations with a record of social impact, supporting business schools to train education leaders, or piloting technology to improve delivery outcomes in remote communities. The report makes little mention of education being an end in itself or a means to transform the world's economic or political structure.

Finally, the report suggests that corporations should work with like-minded businesses, governments, the World Economic Forum, and the Global Partnership for Education, "a multilateral public-private partnership focused on delivering a quality education to all girls and boys." The report provides examples of how the UN has profitably worked alongside corporations such as Hess, Discovery Communication, Sumitomo Chemical, and ING Bank.

In the words of one functionary, the "U.N. considers working with the private sector as a necessity not an option." The UN leadership does not seem concerned that the organization should have different priorities than multinational corporations or that the private sector may prefer to train workers rather than educate citizens to think for themselves.

To further understand the problems with the UN's education agenda, it is worth examining its partnership with the British publishing corporation Pearson.

In *The Smartest Investment,* the UN explains how Pearson drives learning outcomes in Nigeria. Pearson has a $95 million contract with the Lagos State Ministry of Education and the World Bank to develop "measurable solutions" and promote "strong learning outcomes."

To decode this passage, it is useful to turn to a report from the Global Partnership for Education, *Planning for Impact: Measuring Business Investments in Education.* According to this document, businesses want to invest in educational projects with measurable outcomes, such as literacy and numeracy rates and scores on "national and international standardized exams," including the PISA administered by Pearson.

In short, the UN collaborates with Pearson to help Nigeria improve "learning outcomes" as measured by PISA, a Pearson standardized test. Furthermore, the economists Eric A. Hanushek and Ludger Woessman have argued that the UN's education agenda should lead to linking foreign aid to PISA performance. If the UN joins the World Bank in pushing test-based education reform around the world, this idea could come to fruition.

The UN education agenda should not promote the skills agenda, serve multinational corporations, or greenwash investment opportunities. Instead, the UN should recommit to the ideal of humanistic education that recognizes many diverse ways for human beings to learn and to flourish.

Do Not Enter the PISA Testing Race

Education reformers increasingly point to one piece of hard evidence that American schools are failing and in need of shock therapy: PISA scores.

The PISA is a standardized test administered by the Organization for Economic Cooperation and Development (OECD). Every three years, a representative sample of fifteen-year-olds takes the test in approximately seventy countries. The PISA covers reading, math, science, and problem solving; the focus of the 2012 survey was on the capacity to use mathematical concepts in real-world contexts. The ostensible purpose of the PISA is to enable policy makers to gauge how students in their countries are acquiring cognitive skills and to identify high-performing educational systems that may offer useful policy lessons.

The 2012 PISA results for the United States, according to then U.S. secretary of education Arne Duncan, reveal "a picture of educational stagnation" that justifies the need for reforms such as the Common Core educational standards, national tests, value-added teacher evaluations, and charter schools. Other education reformers—including Joel Klein, a former chancellor of New York City schools; Michael Barber, chief education officer of Pearson; and former Florida governor Jeb Bush—have issued similar warnings about the United States's lackluster PISA scores.

While U.S. policy makers should care about the quality of education for American students, they shouldn't place too much value on these scores. In failing to account for factors outside school and by intensifying a testing mentality that educators worldwide increasingly recognize as harmful, the PISA can lead to poor policy recommendations with long-term consequences.

The PISA, of course, has its share of supporters. In their book *Endangering Prosperity: A Global View of the American School,* Stanford economist Eric Hanushek, Harvard political scientist Paul E. Peterson, and German economist Ludger Woessmann make the case for Americans to take the PISA results as seriously as other countries do.

Cognitive human capital, their argument goes, helps determine long-term economic prosperity. And according to them, a math test of fifteen-year-olds provides a reliable indicator of this capital. They write, "Math appears to be the subject in which accomplishment in secondary school is particularly significant for both an individual's and a country's future economic well-being." Furthermore, math is a subject that appears well suited to cross-country comparisons.

On the basis of these scores, advocates argue that American students are performing unsatisfactorily. In 2009, just 32 percent of eighth graders in the United States were deemed proficient in mathematics, and only 7 percent performed at an advanced level. The United States is eighteenth in advanced math achievement, just ahead of the United Kingdom, Italy, Russia, Latvia, Croatia, and Kazakhstan. According to the authors of *Endangering Prosperity,* this is proof that the United States suffers from an "educational malaise" that will be "extremely costly both for the next generation and for the country as a whole."

But there are problems with what the PISA claims to measure and the kinds of policies it supports.

PISA advocates often exaggerate the usefulness of data provided by a test of fifteen-year-olds. For instance, *Endangering Prosperity* projects economic growth rates based on an improvement in PISA test scores. For example, if the United States matches Singapore's score, the average American will earn approximately $300,000 in the year 2085, whereas if the United States reaches only Germany's score, then the average American will earn $150,000. Such projections make too-simple assumptions about eighth-grade test proficiency leading to economic growth and the sustainability of such growth. They also fail to explain how the United States, with its mediocre test scores, has prevailed in the global economy.

Endangering Prosperity also neglects to consider the influence of factors outside school, such as student poverty or wealth. The authors explain that a country's education system has the primary public responsibility for facilitating the acquisition of knowledge and skills. This may be partly true, but according to the OECD, socioeconomically advantaged children perform, on average, the equivalent of one year of formal schooling better than other children. The problem with the United States's PISA scores may be poverty, not the educational system.

Also, the PISA framework can shift educational priorities in a negative way.

The test's advocates offer policy proposals under the banner of education reform. In regard to teacher policy, this means merit pay, the elimination of teacher tenure, and the weakening of teachers' unions. In regard to school choice, it means vouchers, charter schools, and online courses. And in regard to accountability, it means support for annual testing, education standards, and tests for grade promotion or graduation.

But such proposals can unduly burden a country, which must often redesign its whole system to prepare students to excel on standardized tests. The United States began this process with the No Child Left Behind Act and intensified it with President Obama's Race to the Top initiative. As National Public Radio education reporter Anya Kamenetz documents in her new book, *The Test: Why Our Schools Are Obsessed with Standardized Testing—but You Don't Have to Be,* high-stakes standardized tests over the past decade appear to have stunted children's spirit, demoralized teachers, narrowed discussions about education reform to improving scores, and dampened creativity that can lead to economic innovation. "The way much of school is organized around these tests makes little sense for young humans developmentally," she writes. "Nor does it square with what the world needs."

Furthermore, the PISA measures—and thereby incentivizes the teaching of—only a small fraction of what contributes to a meaningful life. Professors Heinz-Dieter Meyer and Katie Zahedi elaborate this point in an open letter to PISA head Andreas Schleicher. "PISA takes attention away from the less measurable or immeasurable educational objectives like physical, moral, civic and artistic development, thereby dangerously narrowing our collective imagination regarding what education is and ought to be," they write. They also worry about the influence of educational corporations affiliated with the PISA that may prioritize making a profit over educational or democratic considerations.

Education reformers seem to want to outdo one another in warning what will happen if the United States does not improve its PISA scores. But such alarmist rhetoric can cloud judgment and lead policy makers to invest limited financial resources in testing rather than education, in designing an educational system geared toward standardized exams rather than nurturing the talents and interests of children.

America's goal should be to provide all children the type of education provided by the finest private schools, with qualified teachers, small classes, sports programs, and a curriculum that includes languages, math, science, history, and the arts. This, more than pushing test scores into the spotlight, will help us out of our educational malaise.

What Brazil Should Know about the Common Core

In spring 2015, more than 155,000 New York students refused to take the Common Core standardized tests. In America, the Obama administration tried to frame opposition to the Common Core as coming from right-wing political extremists or uneducated parents who do not want to hear that their children are not brilliant. According to a Columbia University national survey of test-refusing families, however, many opt-out activists are highly educated and politically liberal. In New York, as in the rest of the country, the test-refusal movement includes progressives and conservatives; people who live in the city, the suburbs, and the country; and families of every ethnicity and race. Despite the best efforts of the federal and state governments, the test-refusal numbers increased in subsequent years.

Many Americans are highly dissatisfied with the Common Core education system. Parents in the test-refusal movement have often heard the arguments for national education standards, standardized tests, and accountability mechanisms. We have heard that this paradigm will prepare all children for college and careers, lift a country's ranking in the PISA, and close the "opportunity gap" between children born into privilege and children born into poverty. Those arguments have a certain appeal, and in 2013, 65 percent of the American public, and 76 percent of teachers, supported the Common Core standards.

By 2015, however, support for the Common Core had plummeted to 49 percent of the American public and 40 percent of teachers. According to one critic, the Common Core is a "lemon"—it looks great but performs poorly and breaks down often. The advertisements for the Common Core are misleading, and many of the problems have become more apparent after the education system has been transformed. Here I offer four reasons why Brazil should rethink its commitment to the National Curricular Common Base.

Bad for Children

In thinking about the question of national education standards, I have found it helpful to use the ideas of John Dewey, arguably America's greatest philosopher of education and democratic

45

political theorist. The first problem Dewey would identify with rigid standards is that they do not consider the needs and desires of the individual student.

In his 1899 essay "The School and Society," Dewey announces a "Copernican revolution" in education whereby "the child becomes the sun around which the appliances of education revolve." According to Dewey, a good teacher discovers and cultivates the interests of each child in the classroom. Dewey thinks that good teachers connect the child's interest with the appropriate curricular materials that will advance the child's knowledge and abilities. As much as possible, skilled educators take advantage of a child's curiosity so that school does not feel like drudgery. In this way, schools teach children that their own thoughts and desires matter and should influence the social world.

National education standards betray Dewey's "Copernican revolution" in education. By stipulating what all children should know by when, policy makers do not allow children to deviate from a one-size-fits-all plan. Performance-pay programs make the problem worse by forcing teachers to stick to the plan or suffer financial loss. In America, wealthy parents have exited the public school system because they do not want their children to be just another number in a standardized system. Children deserve to develop their own singular talents and interests, not just go through a maze designed by distant authority figures.

Bad for Teachers

The second problem with national education standards is that they transfer education decision making out of the school. Top-down education reform comes with costs, including that teachers lose their professional autonomy and children receive an inferior education.

Dewey identified this dynamic in a 1922 speech on "The Classroom Teacher." Policy makers like the idea of giving educators a packaged curriculum and using tests to put teachers and students in line. This factory model is cheap and efficient, and it keeps control in the hands of economic and political elites.

The result, however, is that teachers become uninterested and uninspired. Teaching becomes just a job where you have to do what your boss tells you to do or you will get fired. According to Dewey, teachers only throw themselves into their work with "enthusiasm and wholeheartedness" when they are carrying out plans and ideas that they help develop. The reverse is also the case: people get discouraged when they simply have to follow orders.

Dewey does not concede that standardization makes education better. On the contrary, you cannot expect "creative, independent work from the student when the teachers are still unemancipated." Students know that teachers in this order do not have power to change the plans. As a result, schools become places where teachers and students focus on preparing for standardized tests in a few content areas. This is not a pleasant work space for teachers or an optimal learning environment for students.

Bad for Democracy

The third problem with national education standards is that they reinforce autocratic tendencies in the modern world rather than creating a space for democracy.

Dewey acknowledges that schools need to set flexible, evolving goals for what students learn by a certain time. He calls these goals "aims" and insists that students, teachers, and community members participate in the conversation about what they are. The purpose of these conversations is not merely to map out the curriculum. Rather, the purpose is to create a community where people experience democracy as a living practice rather than merely a means to select leaders.

One school principal expresses Dewey's intuition this way: "School, family, and community must forge their own standards, in dialogue with and in response to the larger world of which they are a part. There will always be tensions; but if the decisive, authoritative voice always comes from anonymous outsiders, then kids cannot learn what it takes to develop their own voice." Dewey thinks schools should teach students *in* democracy, not just *for* democracy; that is, schools should model democracy as a way of life in which ordinary people contribute to the discussion of how to raise the next generation and thereby create a new world.

Local education control empowers many people to run the schools. In a system of national education standards, on the other hand, local authorities, principals, teachers, parents, and students have little power or say over what happens in the school. Schools become a place where everyone in the building learns every day to obey orders or suffer the consequences. It is a lesson in servility.

Bad for the Economy

The fourth problem with national education standards is that they create a docile population and thus lead to lower long-term economic growth.

One scholar who makes this argument is the Chinese scholar Yong Zhao. In his book *World Class Learners,* Zhao explains the secrets to China's success on standardized tests such as the PISA. In China, little outside of schoolwork is valued. Creative and entrepreneurial students either exit the system out of frus-

48

tration with having to do boring, repetitive work or conform to the system's requirements. Chinese students do not spend much time socializing or pursuing their interests or passions. Chinese students lack confidence. According to Zhao, farsighted Chinese policy makers realize that the country needs a different paradigm than the one based on standards and testing.

As an alternative, Zhao looks to the American public school system before the No Child Left Behind Act of 2001. When the American education system was "broken," students pursued extracurricular activities such as music, art, and sports. Children played, by themselves and with others, and often held jobs. American students were happy, confident, and ready to make their own way in the world. As a result of this kind of education, Americans have the world's largest economy, the best colleges and universities on the globe, and a culture that entertains the world.

Zhao thinks that America is making a mistake trying to fix its education system by adopting the Common Core and associated testing. Good standardized test takers do not tend to invent things or start businesses, and "bad" test takers can often be brilliant artists or businesspeople. For Zhao, Brazil should learn the right lessons from China and the United States.

Conclusion

People who advocate national education standards often have good motives, including to educate all children and improve the economy. Brazilians debating the National Curricular Base, however, should learn from America's disastrous experiment with the Common Core. National education standards do not tend to raise the academic bar; instead, they narrow the curriculum to what is tested. They tend to make educators follow scripted lesson plans, make students hate school, and alienate community members, who no longer have a say in what happens in the schools.

National education standards are an expensive, time-consuming distraction from the hard work of educating the next generation. Brazil should look for ways to improve its schools in ways that encourage healthy diversity, community input, teacher autonomy, and student initiative.

American Schools Should Not Teach "Asian Values"

In Westchester County, a suburb of New York City, tutoring businesses are popping up like mushrooms in the forest after a rain. The Kumon Math and Reading Center near the local elementary school, for instance, promises to "give your child the academic advantage to compete in today's world." Unlike the nearby library, theater company, or nature center, this company does not complement the public school curriculum: it simply adds to the test prep that increasingly takes up the day for American children.

What we see in our neighborhood is a result of American policy makers' obsession with test-based education reform. The No Child Left Behind Act of 2001 required all states to test children in math and ELA in grades 3–8 and once in high school. The Race to the Top program of 2009 incentivized states to participate in testing consortia for the Common Core standards in math and ELA. Though the Every Student Succeeds Act of 2015 reverts to the states certain responsibilities about teacher accountability, the law still forces states to "measure the achievement of not less than 95 percent of all students." For the foreseeable future, American children may be stuck taking, or preparing for, standardized tests.

A recurrent explanation for America's focus on testing is that the country needs to emulate Asian education systems. In

2009, U.S. secretary of education Arne Duncan spoke about the results of the PISA. Shanghai, "the jewel of China's education system," ranked number one, while America placed in the middle of the pack. "In a highly-competitive knowledge-based economy, maintaining the educational status quo means America's students are effectively losing ground." According to Duncan, America needs to enter the testing race against Shanghai, Singapore, Hong Kong, Taiwan, Japan, and other countries at the top of the PISA rankings.

At this historical juncture, Americans would do well to listen to Yong Zhao, author of *Who's Afraid of the Big Bad Dragon? Why China Has the Best (and Worst) Education System in the World*. According to Zhao, America is falling into a testing trap that farsighted Chinese are doing their best to exit.

China has the "best" education system in the world, Zhao explains, because parents and students obsess about testing. For over a millennium, Chinese emperors and the Communist Party have built and maintained the *keju,* an educational system that makes testing the primary route to a respectful career. Rather than pursue their own interests, Chinese channel their energies to succeeding at the *gaokao* college admission test. And if the tests gauge memorization of Confucian classics or math abilities, all to the better, for these do not prompt young people to challenge authority.

At the same time, Zhao adds, China has the worst education system in the world, because it "stifles creativity, smothers curiosity, suppresses individuality, ruins children's health, distresses students and parents, corrupts teachers and leaders, and perpetuates social injustice and inequity." Zhao notes that China has failed to produce a Nobel Prize winner, a global cultural icon such as Lady Gaga, or a world-shaping invention in the modern era.

In an article titled "Revisiting Asian Values," the political theorist Leigh Jenco explains the history of the concept of "Asian values." At the end of the nineteenth century, and again at the end of the twentieth, scholars and policy makers identified Asian norms differently from and in opposition to those of Western liberal individualism. Asian values prioritize the community over the individual, harmony over contestation, and rule by appointed experts over popular elections. Jenco thinks there is little to prevent Euro-Americans from adopting these values as their own.

Zhao is not buying the Asian values argument in the context of education. Chinese leaders have designed an educational system upon testing, not for any ethical, educational, or economic reason, but because it trains a docile citizenry. Chinese should not feel bound to agree with the Confucian scholar Mencius that "when Heaven is about to confer a great office on any man, it first exercises his mind with suffering, and his sinews and bones with toil." In practice, Asian values means making kids suffer daily in school—so that, someday, they may be able to make their parents proud.

Zhao encourages Americans to defend the tradition of local control that enabled school districts to dedicate time and resources to drama clubs, sports teams, field trips, and other activities that tap into kids' particular talents and interests. On its old, "broken" education model, America became "the most prosperous and advanced nation in the world." "Erase those values, and you lose the creative power of a culture that celebrates diversity and respects individuality."

In the end, there may not be a way to win a debate about clashing values, any more than you could convince somebody that strong coffee is better than green tea. But many of us wish that an art studio had opened in the place where a business now trains kids to raise test scores.

American Schools Should Not Teach *Grit*

According to the grit narrative, children in the United States are lazy, entitled, and unprepared to compete in the global economy. Schools have contributed to the problem by neglecting socio-emotional skills. The solution, then, is for schools to impart the dispositions that enable American children to succeed in college and careers. According to this story, politicians, policy makers, corporate executives, and parents agree that kids need more grit.

The person who has arguably done more than anyone else to elevate the concept of grit in academic and popular conversations is Angela Duckworth, professor at the Positive Psychology Center at the University of Pennsylvania. In her book *Grit: The Power of Passion and Perseverance,* she explains the concept of grit and how people can cultivate it in themselves and others.

According to Duckworth, grit is the ability to overcome any obstacle in pursuit of a long-term project: "To be gritty is to hold fast to an interesting and purposeful goal. To be gritty is to invest, day after week after year, in challenging practice. To be gritty is to fall down seven times and rise eight." Duckworth names musicians, athletes, coaches, academics, and business-people who succeed because of grit. Her book will be a boon for policy makers who want schools to inculcate and measure grit.

There is a time and place for grit. However, praising grit as such makes no sense because it can often lead to stupid or mean behavior. Duckworth's book is filled with gritty people doing things that they, perhaps, shouldn't.

Take Martin Seligman, the founder of positive psychology and Duckworth's graduate school mentor. In a 1967 article, Seligman and his coauthor describe a series of experiments on dogs. The first day, the dogs are placed in a harness and administered electrical shocks. One group can stop the shocks if they press their noses against a panel, and the other group cannot. The next day, all of the dogs are placed in a shuttle box and again administered shocks that the dogs can stop by jumping over a barrier. Most of the dogs who could stop the shocks the first day jumped over the barrier, while most of the dogs who suffered inescapable shock did not try, though a few did. Duckworth reflects upon this story and her own challenges in a college course in neurobiology. She decides that she passed the course because she would "be like the few dogs who, despite recent memories of uncontrollable pain, held fast to hope." Duckworth would be like one of the dogs that got up and kept fighting.

At no point, however, does Duckworth express concern that many of the animals in Seligman's study died or became ill shortly thereafter. Nor does she note that the CIA may have employed the theory of "learned helplessness" to perform enhanced interrogation, regardless of Seligman's stated opposition to torture. Duckworth acknowledges the possibility that there might be "grit villains" but dismisses this concern because "there are many more gritty heroes." There is no reason to assume this, and it oversimplifies the moral universe to maintain that one has to be a "grit villain" to thoughtlessly harm people.

A second grit paragon in Duckworth's book is Pete Carroll, the Super Bowl–winning coach of the Seattle Seahawks. Carroll has created a culture of grit where assistant coaches chant, "No whining. No complaining. No excuses." She also commends Seahawk defensive back Earl Thomas for playing with "marvellous intensity."

Duckworth has apparently not read any of the articles or seen any of the movies or television programs detailing the long-term harm caused by playing professional football. Barack Obama, among others, has said that he would not want a son, if he had one, to play football. Duckworth might have talked with football players who suffer from traumatic brain injuries.

Another role model, for Duckworth, is Jamie Dimon, the CEO of JPMorgan Chase. Dimon's alma mater prep school has the motto of "Grytte," and Duckworth attributes JPMorgan Chase's success to the grit of its leader: "In the 2008 financial crisis, Jamie steered his bank to safety, and while other banks collapsed entirely, JPMorgan Chase somehow turned a $5 billion profit." There is no basis for the word "somehow" in this sentence. The Troubled Asset Relief Program provided JPMorgan Chase with $25 billion in 2008. In general, neither Duckworth nor the protagonists in her book dwell upon the political conditions that enable or thwart individual success.

Duckworth gives many more troublesome examples: the CEO of Cinnabon, who never reflects on how she contributes to the obesity epidemic in the United States; the Spelling Bee champs who don't love to read; the West Point cadets who have to endure a borderline-hazing initiation rite called Beast.

Why don't these people ever stop to think about what they are doing? We should not celebrate the fact that "paragons of grit don't swap compasses," as Duckworth puts it in her book. That might signal a moral failing on their part. The opposite of grit, often enough, is thinking, wondering, asking questions, and refusing to push a boulder uphill.

Right now, many Americans want the next generation to be gritty. Already, school districts in California are using modified versions of Duckworth's Grit Survey to hold schools and teachers accountable for how well children demonstrate "self-management skills." Duckworth herself opposes grading schools on grit because the measurement tools are unreliable. But that stance overlooks the larger problem of how a grit culture contributes to an authoritarian politics, one where leaders expect the masses to stay on task.

Democracy requires active citizens who think for themselves and, often enough, challenge authority. Consider, for example, what kind of people participated in the Boston Tea Party, the Seneca Falls Convention, the March on Washington, or the present-day test-refusal movement. In each of these cases, ordinary people demand a say in how they are governed. Duckworth celebrates educational models, such as Beast at West Point, that weed out people who don't obey orders. That is a disastrous model for education in a democracy. U.S. schools ought to protect dreamers, inventors, rebels, and entrepreneurs—not crush them in the name of grit.

Pushing Back

Forge Coalitions

I have children in elementary school. As a parent, I have a front-row view of the attempted corporate takeover of America's schools.

The Common Core State Standards Initiative provides a justification for this takeover. The Common Core is a set of educational standards in mathematics and ELA. Many people from across the political spectrum endorse the notion of national education standards. This version of the Common Core, however, has been funded and promoted by groups like the Bill and Melinda Gates Foundation, the Walton Foundation, Exxon, and the U.S. Chamber of Commerce. The Common Core proposes to make students "college and career ready," but corporate interests define what that readiness means.

If a countermovement does not act soon, then the Common Core will impose a neoliberal model of education on America's schools where results, for instance, are measured by standardized test scores.

Fortunately, I am part of several groups contesting the Common Core. Some allies are on the political Left, including Diane Ravitch, who wrote *Reign of Error*, a polemic against the educational privatization movement, and Mark Naison, a colleague at Fordham who helped organize the Badass Teachers Association (BAT). Many people recognize that the Common Core's progressive rhetoric is a Trojan horse for the corporate takeover of schools.

I also work with groups composed largely of self-identified conservatives, such as members of the the Truth in American Education Listserv. Many of the members protest the trend whereby corporations and the U.S. Department of Education, rather than teachers and school boards, determine the standards that drive curriculum and assessment.

I oppose the Common Core because I'm watching it harm my children's school experience. But my personal interests align with my political theoretical ones. I'm a small-*d* democrat and a pluralist. I agree with philosophers like James Madison, J. S. Mill, William E. Connolly, Richard E. Flathman, and Deborah Meier that centralized power facilitates tyranny. Positively stated, I favor political arrangements that distribute power as widely as possible. In the realm of education, I support a variety of educational experiments, including Montessori and Waldorf schools.

In general, I believe in critical thinking, rigor, high education standards, and student and teacher evaluations. Even if I had the power, however, I would not impose one model of education upon the country or define once and for all the key terms in the debate. Intelligent people disagree on how to educate children; it would be foolish to put all of our eggs, so to speak, in one basket.

Proponents of the Common Core sometimes claim that opponents belong to what Paul Krugman calls the "party of stupidity." That is an unfair description of the coalition forming to stop the Common Core.

Here is one map of the current educational landscape:

	POLITICAL LEFT	POLITICAL RIGHT
Centralized Power (Pro-Common Core)	Hillary Clinton; Patty Murray; Democrats for Education Reform	Jeb Bush; Lamar Alexander; ExcelinEd
Distributed Power (Anti-Common Core)	Diane Ravitch; Deborah Meier; Badass Teachers Association	Marco Rubio; Cato Institute; Truth in American Education

To stop the Common Core, citizens need to forge a coalition of people on the political Right and the political Left. In a pluralistic society, citizens need to make alliances with people we agree with on some issues and disagree with on others.

Following are responses to a few potential objections.

Aren't the Common Core just standards? Yes, but that is not the whole story. The Race to the Top program incentivized states to adopt the Common Core standards, aligned tests, and value-added modeling in teacher evaluations. On paper, schools and teachers have flexibility in how or what they teach; in practice, local education authorities are making teachers use Common Core–aligned curricula, including scripted lesson plans or modules. Teachers whose students' scores do not meet the targets on Common Core tests may be fired; school districts whose students do not score highly enough may be taken over by the state.

Does local control mean that schools may teach intelligent design in science classes? The Supreme Court case *Edwards v. Aguillard* (1987) prohibits that.

Might the problem with the Common Core be the execution? Randi Weingarten, the president of the American Federation of Teachers, for instance, supports the idea of the Common Core and argues that the states are failing it. The problem with this line of defense is that it can be used to justify any idea. My school district in Westchester, New York, was thriving before the Common Core and is suffering under it. Some people say that the problem with the Common Core is the high-stakes testing associated with it. Proponents, however, will respond that there needs to be "Big Data" to determine if students are learning the Common Core. The Common Core is the bait to make people adopt much of the corporate education agenda.

Might the Common Core improve the educational standards for some districts? Maybe.

Up to now, however, there is no evidence that the Common Core prepares young children for eventual success in college or careers. There are also stories from around the country (many posted on Diane Ravitch's blog) that students, teachers, and parents hate the Common Core.

The Common Core is a tree that prevents other educational models from getting sunlight. The American educational landscape should be a garden with many flowers.

Prevent Excessive Data Collection

In October 2012, the White House chief technology officer explained what the Big Data revolution entails for education. In remarks to a Datapalooza conference, Todd Walker explained, "You take the data that's already there and jujitsu it, put it in machine-readable form, let entrepreneurs take it and turn it into awesomeness." In colorful prose, Walker expressed the Obama administration's enthusiasm for what Big Data can accomplish in schools. What Walker fails to acknowledge is the dangers posed by Big Data and the need to safeguard children's personal information.

The Promise

Like a lot of Americans, I was captivated by Michael Lewis's *Moneyball,* an account of how the Oakland As in the early 2000s were able to compete with teams with bigger budgets. The key was exploiting market inefficiencies through Big Data. Rather than send scouts to judge players by how they looked, statisticians could calculate whether a batter got on base more frequently than other comparable players. The As let the Yankees spend for big names; the As won by signing unheralded players who mathematically provided the best chance of winning.

Secretary of education Arne Duncan made a similar insight when, in a 2009 speech, he explained the rationale for building Statewide Longitudinal Data Systems: "We want to know whether Johnny participated in an early learning program and completed college on time and whether those things have any bearing on his earnings as an adult." If researchers know that children earn higher incomes when they learn to read at age five rather than six, so the logic goes, then the government has grounds for funding early learning programs. Although education standards and data collection are not necessarily connected, the Race to the Top program entwined the Common Core standards and data systems ostensibly designed to prepare students for colleges and careers.

What Data?

Schools have long collected basic data, such as names, addresses, emergency contacts, and allergies. Federal and state governments have also, in recent decades, required schools to provide data about race, individualized educational programs, and free or reduced-price lunch status. Few people today wish to deny the need for these categories of data collection.

Like the Oakland As, however, Big Data enthusiasts want schools to collect ever more data. According to a December 2013 Fordham Center on Law and Information Policy report, some states now collect data about parental education, pregnancy, birth order, birth weight, medical test results, bullying behavior, and mental health information.

The cutting edge of research and public policy, though, is collecting attitudinal data—that is, information about the inner life of individuals. More precisely, researchers and policy makers want to know whether students have grit.

A February 2013 report by the U.S. Department of Education defines grit as "perseverance to accomplish long-term or higher-order goals in the face of challenges and setbacks." Why measure grit? "Successful students marshal willpower and regulate their attention during such tasks and in the face of distractions." In other words, the U.S. Department of Education wants to know whether students can keep on task or whether they are easily distracted. More precisely, the Education Department wants to know whether students look at the computer and sit in their seats for a long time or whether they look out the window and fidget. The Education Department wants to know if your children like to work or daydream.

Remarkably, the department report on grit does not address much recent scholarship on the benefits of daydreaming, such as the 2012 *Psychological Science* article "Inspired by Distraction: Mind Wandering Facilitates Creative Incubation." The report also barely acknowledges the pernicious political consequences of raising a docile citizenry that rarely wonders if the world could be different.

Collecting Attitudinal Data

In the U.S. Department of Education report on grit, we learn that researchers have designed affective sensors to measure students' blood volume, pulse, and galvanic skin response to determine students' frustration in an online learning environment. We also learn about a mood meter with a camera to detect facial expressions and formulate a smile intensity score.

The science of collecting attitudinal data already exists, including through facial-expression cameras that can be installed on virtually any new computer. The challenge now is how to design systems to collect attitudinal data on a wide, affordable scale.

The Common Core Tests

The Race to the Top program incentivized states to join an assessment consortium, of which there are only two: PARCC and SBAC.

Both testing consortia measure cognitive ability, but SBAC also has said that it may test for attitudinal skills like "time management, goal-setting, self-awareness, persistence, and study skills." Likewise, the president of Achieve, the group that created PARCC, told the New York state assembly in fall 2013 about the need for assessments that "capture digitally the student's test responses and other task-relevant interactive behaviors."

If most American students have to take either the SBAC or PARCC test online, and these tests have the means to measure grit (i.e., persistence in staring at a computer screen), then the United States is much closer to a massive data bank about student attitudes.

The testing consortia have emphasized that all data collection will be subject to the Family Education Rights and Privacy Act of 1974 (FERPA). In January 2012, however, the Education Department revised FERPA to permit "authorized representatives" the power to receive personally identifiable information (PII). For nearly four decades, only educational authorities had access to PII; now, this information may be distributed to government agencies, private nonprofit organizations, research groups, and for-profit companies.

In sum, the Education Department has colluded with the Common Core testing organizations to circumvent the laws against creating a federal student database.

How Does This Affect Homeschoolers?

In *The Prince,* Machiavelli observes that when fevers are hard to discern, they are easier to cure than when the fever is manifest. In other words, astute political actors need to be ready for events before and as they unfold.

Homeschoolers have long been required to take state exams in math and English. At the time of writing, I have not found evidence that states are requiring homeschooled students to take the grades 3–8 PARCC or SBAC test. Homeschoolers should anticipate, however, legislators and educational agencies demanding that children take these tests to prove they are becoming college and career ready.

The task, then, is to contest data acquisition of attitudinal data, including through the PARCC or SBAC test or whatever may replace the tests down the road. In the short term, that means entering the current political debates about whether states should pay the astronomical costs to build the technological infrastructure to support the PARCC and SBAC tests.

The government does not have the right to know whether our children daydream. The time for parents to fight for their children's right to privacy is now.

Take Up the Civil Rights Legacy

Given the power of its symbolism, many individuals and entities have attempted to appropriate the legacy of the civil rights

movement for their own purposes. In 2010, for instance, con-
servative talk show host Glenn Beck led a march on Washington
to restore what he professed was the distorted history of the
movement. While Beck's tenuous appeal to the movement's
heritage might be dismissed, the danger of misappropriation
of its core values of justice and equality are greater when the
person or group doing the usurping can legitimately lay a claim
to that legacy.

This has become clear with a 2014 campaign to promote the
Common Core State Standards by the National Urban League,
which played an important if less visible role during the civil rights movement. Marc H. Morial, president of the National
Urban League, has declared that the Common Core will "help
bridge the achievement gap by leveling the playing field so that
all students, regardless of race, geography or income, have an
equal shot at gaining the knowledge and skills necessary to succeed in the 21st century global economy." The National Urban
League partnered with Radio One to deliver this message on
multiple media platforms.

Education should empower young men and women, of whatever race or background, to succeed in college and careers. The
Common Core's promise, however, does not correspond to its
reality. More strongly, the Common Core betrays the civil rights
legacy more than advancing it.

In his book on the origin and consequences of No Child Left
Behind, *An Education in Politics,* the political scientist Jesse H.
Rhodes explains why civil rights activists support the idea of
national education standards. For years, activists demanded
that black children have the same opportunities as white children, including science and history courses, music and theater
programs, and qualified teachers running small classes. The equity movement failed, however, to produce measurable results
and overcome conservative opposition.

The idea of educational standards, however, unites civil rights and business groups convinced that all Americans need a quality education. That is why both the National Urban League and the U.S. Chamber of Commerce support the Common Core. The excellence movement, as it is called, may succeed where the equity movement didn't.

Yet good intentions do not always translate into effective policies. The National Urban League, whose mission is to "enable African Americans to secure economic self-reliance, parity, power and civil rights," is on shaky ground with the Common Core. There are at least three reasons why the Common Core is already harming a generation of young African Americans.

First and foremost, Common Core testing has branded a large percentage of black youth as failures. In New York, only 19.3 percent of black students demonstrated proficiency on state math tests, and 17.6 percent demonstrated proficiency on state ELA tests. Do these numbers light a fire under educators to do a better job? Maybe. But they also mean that the educational system is signaling to many black children that they have no future in higher education or the modern workforce.

Second, the Common Core focuses attention on math and English test prep above all other academic or extracurricular pursuits. The Race to the Top program incentivized states to adopt the Common Core as well as a testing regime that punishes teachers or schools with low student test scores. In New York City, the Success Academy charter schools excel on the Common Core tests. How? According to one administrator, they do so by turning children into "little test-taking machines." It goes without saying that many wealthy parents would never accept such an education for their children; in practice, the Common Core widens rather than narrows the opportunity gap.

Finally, the Common Core dedicates limited resources to textbook and testing companies rather than teachers and children. The Race to the Top program awarded $330 million to two Common Core testing consortia: PARCC and SBAC. Schools, in turn, must purchase aligned curricula as well as the technology to run the online Common Core tests. Meanwhile, financially strapped school districts are cutting art and music programs that stimulate brain development and teach skills such as cooperation and perseverance. This is a disaster for all students, including African American ones.

Even if one shares the National Urban League's ambition to prepare black youth to succeed in the twenty-first-century global economy, the Common Core is not the way to make that happen. So far, the Common Core is draining educational budgets, narrowing the curriculum, and turning students into test-taking robots. This is no way to advance the civil rights legacy. Instead, the country should recommit to the principle that all children, of whatever race or background, can attain the same kind of education only available, right now, to the children of privilege.

Refuse the Tests

In spring 2014, thousands of students refused to take the Common Core ELA exams. In New York, as in states across the country, parents told administrators that their children would not sit for exams that pressure teachers to teach to the test and drain school budgets.

Ignore the baseless charge that families don't want high academic standards for their kids or are afraid their kids won't live up to higher standards. Parents and students want schools that offer a well-rounded curriculum and a sensible amount and way of testing. But the Common Core has transformed much of public education into preparing for and taking standardized tests.

According to the *2014 New York Testing Program School Administrator's Manual,* parents may eventually review students' responses to open-ended questions, but they are not allowed to look at the test itself. Although educators are under a gag order from New York State and Pearson that prohibits them from discussing specifics of the tests, Principal Elizabeth Phillips of PS 321 in Park Slope, Brooklyn, and other educators across the state have decried the ELA exams as confusing and developmentally inappropriate.

The situation may be the same in mathematics. Stanford professor James Milgram argues that the Common Core math standards do not command international respect and will not prepare students for STEM careers. If the state keeps hiding the exams from public scrutiny, then parents and educators have a right to doubt their pedagogical value.

There are other issues. The Race to the Top program awarded New York $700 million on the condition that the state adopt a value-added modeling (VAM) teacher evaluation system, in this case, APPR. Put plainly, the state may now fire teachers if test scores are low. That creates incredible pressure to teach to the test.

Additionally, English language learners must take the tests, regardless of how well they can understand them, and teachers in impoverished school districts are more likely to be punished, despite taking on harder assignments. In the words of noted education scholar Diane Ravitch, VAM is a sham.

In spring 2014, I attended an iRefuse rally held on Long Island. The poster for the event juxtaposes two silhouettes of a child's head: one, under the title "Learning," is filled with images of Shakespeare, a guitar, a flower, math equations, and plants; the other, under the title "Testing," is filled with a multiple-choice exam. That is why parents are refusing—they want school to be a place where children's talents are cultivated and not harmed by tests whose main use is to fire teachers.

In 1849, the American philosopher Henry David Thoreau wrote a classic essay on civil disobedience that has inspired countless activists around the world, including Mahatma Gandhi and Martin Luther King Jr. According to Thoreau, "it is not desirable to cultivate a respect for the law, so much as for the right." According to Thoreau, people are too inclined to respect the government rather than question whether the people who lead it are acting justly.

A parent inspired by Thoreau would object to the *School Administrators Manual*'s policy that "schools do not have any obligation to provide an alternative location or activities for individual students while the tests are being administered." This sentence justifies the sit-and-stare policy whereby refusing children are not allowed to read or talk but are forced to remain at their desks while their peers take the tests. In other words, this manual encourages administrators to employ the "silent treatment" on kids who don't want their education to become endless test prep. This is bullying pure and simple.

As a parent, what should you do regarding your child's participation in high-stakes Common Core tests? Write a letter or email to the board of education, superintendent, principals, and teachers in your school district to formally notify them of your decision on behalf of your child to refuse the tests.

There is a chance that administrators will try to dissuade you. Tell them that you are advocating for your children to receive a well-rounded, personalized education. Tell everyone in your district that you are not fighting him or her but rather political and corporate forces that are trying to centralize and standardize public education.

Don't Be Fooled by Rebranding

In a speech in Washington in early 2018, secretary of education Betsy DeVos called the education standards known as the Common Core a "disaster" and proclaimed, "At the U.S. Department of Education, Common Core is dead."

The reality, however, is that the Common Core is still very much alive. As indicated in a November 2017 report from Achieve, twenty-four states have "reviewed and revised" their English and math standards under the Common Core. In some instances, such as in New York, the revised standards are known by a different name.

This is worth pointing out because the Common Core has soured many people on public education and civic life in general. When one group of people decides the national education standards, other people feel alienated from the schools and the democratic process.

Many families oppose the Common Core and have refused the associated end-of-year tests, such as the PARCC, SBAC, ACT Aspire, or New York State Common Core 3–8 English Language Arts and Mathematics Tests. Critics argue that Common Core math expects students to justify their answers in ways that are "unnecessary and tedious." Others note that the standards will not prepare many students to major in a STEM discipline in college. And for some scholars and parents, the "close textual reading" under Common Core makes learning a chore rather than a pleasure.

In 2013, then secretary of education Arne Duncan said the Common Core may "prove to be the single greatest thing to happen to public education in America since *Brown v. Board of Education*." For Duncan and others, the Common Core promised to prepare all students to succeed in college, career, and life.

But that view did not align with popular support for the Common Core, which dropped from 83 percent to 50 percent between 2013 and 2016. For many parents and educators, the Common Core has made public education worse.

For critics like author and former assistant secretary of education Diane Ravitch, the Common Core is "fundamentally flawed" because of the way the standards were developed. Common Core work group members included more people from the testing industry than experienced teachers, subject-matter experts, or early-childhood educators. According to some early-childhood health and education professionals, the standards conflict with research about how children learn and how best to teach them.

When President Obama signed the Every Student Succeeds Act in 2015, Senator Lamar Alexander (R-Tenn.) stated that the Republican congressional majority had "kept its promise to repeal the federal Common Core mandate."

As a candidate for president, Donald J. Trump tweeted how he had been consistent in his opposition to the Common Core and argued that the federal government should "get rid of Common Core—keep education local!"

It seemed only a matter of time before many states would move away from the Common Core.

As of 2018, however, nearly every state that adopted the Common Core during the Obama administration has kept the most important features. Across the country, children will study for and take end-of-year tests that align with the Common Core.

Alexander's claim that Congress has repealed the Common Core mandate is misleading. The federal government has made it an expensive gamble for states to adopt education standards that differ from the Common Core.

According to the Every Student Succeeds Act, states that wish to adopt an alternative to the Common Core must now prove to the secretary of education that the standards are "challenging."

According to the law, "each state shall demonstrate that the challenging state academic standards are aligned with entrance requirements for credit-bearing coursework in the system of public higher education in the State." Most states adopted the Common Core as part of their Race to the Top applications during the Obama administration. Race to the Top gave an incentive to states to align high school graduation requirements and college entrance requirements with the new standards. States that keep the Common Core do not have to change anything to satisfy this provision. States that adopt new standards must prove to the secretary that high school graduates will be able to take credit-bearing courses as soon as they enter a public college or university.

In addition, the law requires states to adopt standards that align with "relevant State career and technical education standards." The main Common Core reading standards are called the "college and career readiness anchor standards." For states that want to meet this criterion of the law, the safest bet is to keep the Common Core.

States have a strong financial incentive to meet these criteria. The Every Student Succeeds Act directs approximately $22 billion a year to states around the country, including more than $700 million to Ohio, $1.6 billion to New York, $2 billion to Texas, and $2.6 billion to California. If a state fails to meet any of the requirements of the law, "the Secretary may withhold funds for State administration under this part until the Secretary determines that the State has fulfilled those requirements."

Secretary DeVos has approved virtually all plans that include the Common Core or a slightly modified version. According to *Education Week,* even when states have revised the standards, "the core of the Common Core remains."

What's the Alternative? John Dewey's Vision

DID YOU ATTEND A PUBLIC SCHOOL in the United States and perform in a school play, take field trips, or compete on a sports team? Did you have a favorite teacher who designed his own curriculum, say, about the Civil War, or helped you find your particular passions and interests? Did you take classes that were not academic per se but that still opened your eyes to different aspects of human experience, such as fixing cars? Did you do projects that required planning and creativity? If the answer to any of these questions is yes, then you are the beneficiary of John Dewey's pedagogical revolution.

In 1916, Dewey put forth the philosophy of education that would change the world in *Democracy and Education*. Dewey's influence is far-reaching, but his pedagogy has been under assault for at least a generation. The National Commission on Excellence in Education report *A Nation at Risk* (1983) signaled the rise of the anti-Dewey front, under the somewhat misleading name of the "education reform" movement. The report warned that other countries would soon surpass the United States in wealth and power because "a rising tide of mediocrity" had engulfed U.S. schools. The problem, according to the report, is that U.S. education is "an often incoherent, out-dated patchwork quilt." The education reform movement aims to replace that "patchwork quilt"—mostly made by local school boards, teachers, and parents—with a more uniform system based on national standards.

The political Right has often led the charge against Dewey's legacy. In 1897, Dewey described his "pedagogic creed" as "in-dividualistic" and "socialistic" because it sees the need to nur-ture each child's unique talents and interests in a supportive community. For both the business community and traditional-values conservatives, Dewey's pedagogy fails to train work-ers and inculcates liberal, even socialistic, values. The U.S. Chamber of Commerce and the Charles Koch–funded con-servative think tank the Heartland Institute, to take just two examples, have tried to purge the U.S. education system of its progressive elements. Similarly, in 2002, President George W. Bush signed the No Child Left Behind Act, an anti-Deweyan measure requiring states to implement test-based education reform.

The education reform movement has been successful, how-ever, because many Democrats are also enthusiastic partici-pants. In 1989, Bill Clinton, then governor of Arkansas, orga-nized the education summit at the University of Virginia that began the process of formulating national education stan-dards. Senator Ted Kennedy encouraged Democratic mem-bers of Congress to vote for No Child Left Behind. In 2009, the Obama administration ran the Race to the Top competitive grant program that incentivized states to adopt the Common Core standards in mathematics and English. Former secretary of state and presidential candidate Hillary Clinton supports the Common Core and many other planks of education re-form. Today, few Democrats with a national profile speak up for Dewey's ideal of progressive education.

74

Why does this matter? Progressive education teaches children to pursue their own interests and exercise their voices in their communities. In the twentieth century, these kinds of young people participated in the movements against the Vietnam War and for civil rights. They founded Greenpeace and Students for a Democratic Society, listened to the Beatles and attended Woodstock, and established artistic communities and organic groceries. Though Dewey was not a beatnik, a hippy, or a countercultural figure himself, his philosophy of education encourages young people to fight for a world where everyone has the freedom and the means to express her own personality. The education reform movement is not just about making kids take standardized tests; it is about crushing a rebellious spirit that often gives economic and political elites a headache.

For those who think that democracy ought to be a way of life rather than merely a means to select leaders, and that schools serve a vital civic function of teaching children to become autonomous adults, now is the time to recover the vision Dewey outlined in *Democracy and Education*. The book presents an inspiring vision of children learning to express their individuality in ways that enrich the community. Dewey teaches us that children learn about democracy by watching educators and citizens make important decisions within their schools rather than by following orders from above. He also shows us how education progressives can sometimes win even if, as is the case now, reformers have the ear of the wealthy and powerful.

Born in 1859 in Burlington, Vermont, Dewey earned his doctorate at Johns Hopkins University in Baltimore before beginning an academic career primarily at two institutions: the University of Chicago and Columbia University in New York. At the beginning of his career, Dewey grappled with the problem of how to reconcile absolute idealism and philosophical naturalism. On one hand, he shared Hegel's aspiration to overcome the divisions that separate the individual from the community, the brain from the hand, and the head from the heart. On the other, he thought that Charles Darwin's work prompted philosophers to rethink fundamental presuppositions, including whether reason is a pure faculty or rather a way to describe human intelligence imperfectly navigating the material world. Dewey's work in the early part of his career was dedicated to thinking through this challenge in order to arrive at a doctrine variously called *instrumentalism, functionalism,* or *pragmatism.*

In 1894, however, Dewey faced a dilemma that gave a new purpose to his philosophical career: choosing a school for his children. In a letter to his wife, Alice, Dewey wrote, "When you think of the thousands and thousands of young ones who are practically ruined negatively if not positively in the Chicago schools every year, it is enough to make you go out and howl on the street corners like the Salvation Army." Shortly thereafter, Dewey helped to open the Laboratory School of the University of Chicago, where Alice subsequently worked as a teacher and principal, and which four of his own children attended.

For Dewey, however, it was not enough to ensure that his own children received a good education. He maintained that the future of democracy hinged on offering a well-rounded, personalized education to all children and not just those of the wealthy, intelligent, or well connected. Dewey's pedagogic creed is that "education is the fundamental method of social progress and reform." Schools could teach students and communities to exercise autonomy and make democracy a concrete reality. The very name "Laboratory School" suggests that Dewey wanted the ideas developed there to be disseminated among education researchers and policy makers. What was un-acceptable was a two-tiered education system that reinforced class and racial divisions.

Dewey's vision brought him into conflict with industrialists and administrators who thought that schools should primarily prepare the vast majority of the population for the workforce. In 1915, Dewey had a public exchange in the pages of the *New Republic* with David Snedden, the commissioner of education for Massachusetts. Snedden argued that public schools should train children for the types of jobs that they would be likely to do once they graduated. Dewey responded that vocational ed-ucation should not "adapt" workers to the economy but rather teach kids how things work so that they could lay the ground for an industrial democracy. The Smith–Hughes Act (1917) and the Cardinal Principles of Secondary Education (1918) enacted laws and policies that seem to support Snedden's vision of vo-cational education for the masses.

Dewey and the progressive movement, however, won a crucial concession from the vocational education movement. Snedden wanted separate schools for the college bound and for those destined to work on farms or in factories. What transpired, instead, was that public schools added woodwork-ing shops and garages to teach automotive technology and the like. This compromise partially realized Dewey's vision. Philosophically, Dewey sought to overcome the dualism be-tween the mind and the body, and, pedagogically, he sought to bring the liberal arts and vocational education into closer con-tact. Though Dewey opposed efforts to track kids from an early age, he wanted schools to be places where kids from different backgrounds and with diverse interests could meet and talk with one another.

Dewey's philosophy exercised a profound impact on U.S. education in the mid-twentieth century. One reason is that many powerful individuals and groups advocated his ideas, including at Teachers College, Columbia University, as well as at the Progressive Education Association, at the U.S. Office of Education, and at state departments of education. Dewey's influence peaked during the "Great Compression," the decades after the Second World War when the middle class had the clout to say that what is good for wealthy people's kids is what is good for their own. In *Democracy and Education,* Dewey envisioned schools "equipped with laboratories, shops and gardens, where dramatisations, plays and games are freely used." If a public school has a gymnasium, an art studio, a garden, a playground, or a library, then one can see Dewey's handiwork.

In 1985, a few scholars wrote a book called *The Shopping Mall High School* to deride the tendency in the United States to offer a wide array of courses, many of which have a tenuous connection to academic subjects. For Dewey, however, the other side of this story is that schools and communities were trying to find ways to engage children. As we shall see, Dewey did not think that schools should simply pander to children's current interests. At the same time, he opposed efforts to impose a ready-made curriculum on children across the country— or, more pointedly, on those whose parents could not afford to send them to private schools.

Dewey wrote *Democracy and Education* based upon his lectures at Teachers College. The book is, technically, a textbook, and it contains useful advice for teachers and administrators. He also said that the book "was for many years that in which my philosophy, such as it was, was most fully expounded." Dewey's philosophy lays the foundation for his pedagogy and ensures that his book is still worth reading over a century after publication, yet his philosophical style also puts a barrier between many readers and the actionable ideas. We might lower that barrier by exploring the meaning and significance of one of the key themes of *Democracy and Education,* namely, that school should be interesting for children.

According to Dewey, all children enter the classroom with interests. "To take an interest is to be on the alert, to care about, to be attentive." Children care about their families, their neighborhoods, and their own lives. They also can become interested in new things under the right circumstances. Dewey's concept of interest has analogies to Hegel's concept of *Geist* (spirit), as both are at the core of one's being and expressive of a larger entity. But one does not need to be a scholar of German idealism to grasp Dewey's point that different children become "alive" when doing some things and not others.

The task of the teacher, according to Dewey, is to harness the child's interest to the educational process. "The problem of instruction is thus that of finding material which will engage a person in specific activities having an aim or purpose of moment or interest to him." Teachers can employ Dewey's insight by having a pet rabbit in the classroom. As students take care of the animal, and watch it hop about the classroom, they become interested in a host of topics: how to feed animals, the proper care of animals, the occupation of veterinarians, and biology. Rather than teach material in an abstract manner to young children, a wise teacher brings the curriculum into "close quarters with the pupil's mind."

According to Dewey, teachers should cultivate a student's natural interest in the flourishing of others. It is a mistake to interpret interest as self-interest. Our thriving is intimately connected with the flourishing of other people. The role of democratic education is to help children see their own fate as entwined with that of the community's, to see that life becomes richer if we live among others pursuing their own interests. Democracy means equitably distributed interests. All children—rich, poor, black, white, male, female, and so forth—should have the opportunity to discover and cultivate their interests. Schools ought to be the site where we model a society that reconciles individualism and socialism and that allows each child to add her own distinct voice to society's choir.

What is controversial about Dewey's concept of interest? Sometimes, far-right groups share the following quote attributed to Dewey: "Children who know how to think for themselves spoil the harmony of the collective society, which is coming, where everyone is interdependent." There is no factual basis for this attribution, and for good reason: it contravenes Dewey's ambition to achieve a higher synthesis between strong-willed individuals and a democratic society, not to crush a child's individuality for the sake of social uniformity. Dewey makes this point crystal clear in his essay "The School and Society" (1899), where he announces a Copernican revolution in education whereby "the child becomes the sun about which the appliances of education revolve."

Here, then, we understand the explosive core of Dewey's philosophy of education. He wants to empower children to think for themselves and cooperate with each other. The purpose of widely distributing interests is to break down "barriers of class, race, and national territory" and "secure to all the wards of the nation equality of equipment for their future careers." Imagine a world without racism or sexism, one where all children get the same kind of education as the wisest and wealthiest parents demand for their own children, and one that trains workers to question whether their interests are being served by the current ownership and use of the means of production. Dewey is the spiritual head of the New Left, whose writings have both inspired teachers and infused schools—and provoked a reaction from those who detest this political vision.

A perennial critique of Dewey's philosophy of education is that it does not adequately introduce children to Western civilization or the rigors of scientific thinking. In "The Crisis in Education," the German philosopher Hannah Arendt decries "the bankruptcy of progressive education." Though she does not mention Dewey by name, she suggests that his ideas "completely overthrew, as though from one day to the next, all traditions and all the established methods of teaching and learning." Decades later, the American educator E. D. Hirsch Jr. argued in *Cultural Literacy* (1987) that Dewey is a Rousseauian Romantic who thinks that children can be trusted to teach themselves everything they need to know. However, according to Hirsch, "Tarzan is a pure fantasy," and what children need to do is learn key ideas and facts about our culture—which, conveniently, he includes in an appendix to his book. More recently, the Common Core claims to cure the problem that the U.S. curriculum has tended to be "a mile wide and an inch deep."

All of these assaults on Dewey misrepresent his philosophy. Dewey always retained Hegel's ethical ideal of reconciling opposites to achieve a higher synthesis. In his essay "The Child and the Curriculum" (1902), he explains why it is essential to keep both things in mind when designing and running schools.

Dewey believes that educators need to place themselves in the mind of the child, so to speak, to determine how to begin his education journey. "An end which is the child's own carries him on to possess the means of its accomplishment." Many parents who take their families to children's museums are acting upon this idea. A good museum will teach children for hours without them ever becoming conscious of learning as such. Climbing through a maze gives children opportunities to solve problems; floating vessels down an indoor stream teaches children about water and hydrodynamics; building a structure with bricks and then placing it on a rumbling platform introduces children to architecture—all of these activities make learning a joy.

For Dewey, however, it is essential that educators lead children on a considered path to the cutting edge of scientific knowledge on a multitude of topics. A good teacher will place stimuli in front of children that will spark their imagination and inspire them to solve the problem at hand. The goal is to incrementally increase the challenges so that students enter what the Russian psychologist Lev Vygotsky in the 1920s called the "zone of proximal development," where they stretch their mental faculties. At a certain point, children graduate from museums and enter a more structured curriculum. There can be intermediary or supplementary steps—say, when they make a business plan, learn to sail, or intern at an architect's office. Eventually, teachers have to rely on traditional methods of reading, lecturing, and testing to make sure that students learn the material.

In the conclusion to "The Child and the Curriculum," Dewey enjoins, "Let the child's nature fulfil its own destiny, revealed to you in whatever of science and art and industry the world now holds as its own." He has faith that the child's nature will find expression in the highest forms of human endeavor and that, for example, a kindergarten artist might grow into an accomplished painter. Dewey also believes that individual expression tends to lead to socially beneficial activities. These articles of faith are not necessarily vindicated by experience. Sometimes children choose the wrong path, and sometimes well-educated individuals seek to profit from other people's misery.

For Dewey, however, democracy requires running the risk that all children, and not just those of the wealthy or connected, deserve a well-rounded education. Dewey wants schools to teach children to think for themselves and act in ways that benefit the community. He envisions a society where each person can express herself in a manner that enriches everyone—in the way that an orchestra harnesses the gifts of its members or a potluck becomes more fun when many people bring their signature dishes. Dewey's vision inspired generations of teachers and parents and, for a few decades, shaped education policy. It would be a tragedy for the schools, and our democracy, if we were to give it up for the paltry vision of an education model based on standardized tests.

Looking around the contemporary political landscape, it is easy to become despondent about the prospects of progressive education. Economic and political elites agree on the main elements of so-called education reform. Parents and teachers have been fighting back, but they don't have nearly the same political connections or economic might.

Dewey, however, also provides guidance for how progressives can win victories in education policy. Americans still believe in the ideal of democracy. No matter how much power education reformers get at the top of the political order, they still need support from the population for the reforms to stick. The Bill and Melinda Gates Foundation, for instance, has spent millions of dollars trying to prop up support for the Common Core even as public opinion shows widespread disillusionment with the standards. Despite their money and power, education reformers are scared by the parent-led movement to refuse the Common Core standardized tests. They should be.

Dewey shows us that appeals to democracy carry weight. We recoil at the notion that some children deserve a better education than others because of their parents' political or economic status. Nobody will say with a straight face that wealthy children should be raised to lead, while middle- or lower-class children are raised to follow, or that the kind of education available at the finest private schools should be an exclusive privilege of those born with silver spoons in their mouths. "What the best and wisest parent wants for his own child, that must the community want for all of its children. Any other ideal for our schools is narrow and unlovely; acted upon, it destroys our democracy." Dewey's words ring as true today as they did a century ago. In the face of the unrelenting attack of the education reform movement, we must fight to actualize Dewey's vision of great schools providing the foundation for a living democracy.

Acknowledgments

I thank my friends, editors, and fellow education activists with whom I have discussed the ideas in this book (apologies to those whom I have neglected to mention): Aaron Jaffe, Aixa Rodriguez, Allison White, Arthur Goldstein, Beth Dimino, Bianca Tanis, Bonnie Beyer, Carol Anne, Carol Burris, Chris Cerrone, Christel Swasey, Christine Zirkelbach, Damon Buffum, Dave Greene, David Johnson, Deborah Brooks, Deborah Meier, Diane Livingston, Diane Ravitch, Edith Baltazar, Edward Ra, Frank Schnecker, Gail Richmond, Gary Lamb, Gary Stern, George Latimer, Glen Dalgleish, Greg Britton, Jamaal Abdul-Alim, Jamaal Bowman, Jeanette Deutermann, Jennifer Fall, Jia Lee, Johann Neem, Julia Rubin, Julie Borst, Karen Braun, Katie Lapham, Katie Zahedi, Kevin Kelly, Kirsten Lombard, Kristin Smith, Laura Mazziotti, Leonie Haimson, Linda Monk, Lisa Litvin, Lisa Rudley, Liz O'Shea, Lori Koerner, Luz Mooney, Mark Naison, Marla Kilfoyle, Marla Schneider, Megan Kilpatrick, Mercedes Schneider, Michael Hynes, Michael Lillis, Mindy Rosier, Nate Morgan, Patrice Maynard, Peter Greene, Priscilla Sanstead, Rebecca Hegenauer, Sam Haselby, Sarah Blaine, Shane Vander Hart, Shannon Joy, Shenila Khoja-Moolji, Susan Polos, Susan Ochshorn, Susan Watson, Suzanne Coyle, Terry Kalb, Tiffany

Dunn, Tim Farley, Tim Macdowall, Tricia Farmer, William Germano, Yohuru Williams, Yvonne Gasperino, and Zephyr Teachout.

Publication History

"Kindergarten, Disrupted" was originally published as "Do We Need a Common Core?," *Huffington Post,* May 7, 2012. http://www.huffingtonpost.com/.

"The Common Core Curriculum and Scripted Lesson Plans" was originally published as "Why Are Parents Revolting against the Common Core? Start with the English Curriculum," *Huffington Post,* January 16, 2014. http://www.huffingtonpost.com/.

"Bill Gates, Bankroller of the Common Core" was originally published as "Bill Gates Should Not Micro-manage Our Schools," *SchoolBook,* May 17, 2013. http://www.wnyc.org/.

"David Coleman, Architect of the Common Core" was originally published as "David Coleman's Plan to Destroy Education," *Al Jazeera America,* December 5, 2014. http://america.aljazeera.com/.

"Michael Barber, Pearson Deliverologist" was originally published as "For Pearson, Common Core Is Private Profit," *Al Jazeera America,* March 24, 2015. http://america.aljazeera.com/.

"How Democratic Party Elites Educate Their Own Kids" was originally published as "Democratic Party Elites Have Abandoned Public Education," *Al Jazeera America,* August 21, 2015. http://america.aljazeera.com/.

"How Obama and Congress Cemented the Common Core" was originally published as "Congress and Obama Feign a Course Correction on Testing," *Al Jazeera America,* December 8, 2015. http://america.aljazeera.com/.

"The English Language Arts Standards Stifle Thought " was originally published as "Thinking in School," Hannah Arendt Center, January 19, 2015. http://www.hannaharendtcenter.org/.

"The Math Standards Do Not Prepare Children for STEM Majors or Careers" was originally published as "The Problem with the Common Core Math Standards," *Huffington Post,* October 31, 2013. http://www.huffingtonpost.com/.

"The Next Generation Science Standards Lead to Computer Simulations, Not Hands-On Tasks" was originally published as "Corporate Science Standards Not Best for School," *Journal News,* December 19, 2016. http://www.lohud.com/.

"The College Board's Interest in Advanced Placement U.S. History" was originally published as "College Board Shouldn't Monopolize How US History Is Taught," *Al Jazeera America,* October 7, 2014. http://america.aljazeera.com/.

"The United Nations's Problematic Education Agenda" was originally published as "Corporate Education Reform Goes Global," *Al Jazeera America,* January 26, 2016. http://america.aljazeera.com/.

"Do Not Enter the PISA Testing Race" was originally published as "Don't Make a Mountain out of PISA Scores," *Al Jazeera America,* January 22, 2015. http://america.aljazeera.com/.

"What Brazil Should Know about the Common Core" was originally published as "Por que os padrões nacionais de educação são uma má ideia," *Patio* (Brazil), March/May 2017. http://loja.grupoa.com.br/.

"American Schools Should Not Teach 'Asian Values'" was originally published as "Education Reform and Asian Values," *E-International Relations,* December 24, 2015. http://www.e-ir.info/.

"American Schools Should Not Teach 'Grit'" was originally published as "Teaching 'Grit' Is Bad for Children, and Bad for Democracy," *Aeon,* June 2, 2016. https://aeon.co/.

"Forge Coalitions" was originally published as "Forging Coalitions to Stop the Common Core," *The Contemporary Condition,* December 12, 2013. http://contemporarycondition.blogspot.com/.

"Prevent Excessive Data Collection" was originally published as "Who Should Know That Your Child
Daydreams?," *The Homeschool Handbook,* July/August 2014.
http://www.thehomeschoolhandbook.com/.

"Take Up the Civil Rights Legacy" was originally published as
"Common Core Betrays the Civil Rights Movement," coauthored with
Yohuru Williams, *Truthout,* November 5, 2014. Copyright Truthout.org.
Reprinted with permission.

"Refuse the Tests" was originally published as "Why Common
Core Tests Are Bad," CNN, April 23, 2014. CNN retains the rights.
http://www.cnn.com/.

"Don't Be Fooled by Rebranding" was originally published as "Betsy
DeVos Said Common Core Was 'Dead'—It's Not," *The Conversation,*
March 26, 2018. https://theconversation.com/.

"What's the Alternative? John Dewey's Vision" was originally published as "In Praise of Dewey," *Aeon,* July 28, 2016. https://aeon.co/.

(Continued from page ii)

FORERUNNERS: IDEAS FIRST